The
Afternoon
of
Life

FINDING PURPOSE AND
JOY IN MIDLIFE

The
Afternoon
of Life

FINDING PURPOSE AND
JOY IN MIDLIFE

ELYSE FITZPATRICK

P U B L I S H I N G
P.O. BOX 817 • PHILLIPSBURG • NEW JERSEY 08865-0817

Page design and typesetting by Lakeside Design Plus

Printed in the United States of America

Library of Congress Cataloging-in-Publication Data
Fitzpatrick, Elyse, 1950–
    The afternoon of life : finding purpose and joy in midlife / Elyse Fitzpatrick.
       p. cm.
    Includes bibliographical references (p.).
    ISBN 0-87552-197-5 (paper)
    1. Christian women—Religious life. 2. Middle aged women—Religious life. I. Title.

BV4579.5.F58 2004
248.8'43—dc22

                            2004044555

Dedication

To my darlings:
Wesley David, Hayden Dexter,
Eowyn Elyse, and Alexandria Louise—
thank you for the joy you've brought to
this afternoon woman's heart.

Contents

Acknowledgments

Heartfelt thanks need to go to Barbara Lerch of P&R Publishing for her diligent and patient encouragement of me during this project. My appreciation also goes out to the members of my church (Grace Church, SGM) and particularly my small-group members who have prayed for me through this project. The wonderful women in my book club (The Swans) have also been a great inspiration to me, particularly as they have wrestled through deep theology and applied it to all the seasons in their lives. Thank you so much for your help.

Thanks also to my family, who have made my afternoon years truly golden, particularly my dear life-friend and husband, Phil; our lovely children (James, Jessica, and Joel) and their spouses (Cody and Ruth) and their children (a.k.a. my darlings). Thank you all so much for your love and prayers. And thanks again to my mom, Rosemary, for her input and edits to the manuscript. You're a truly valiant woman.

Introduction

The "afternoon of life" is a phrase that I first used in Women Helping Women.[1] *In America, the average woman's life expectancy is seventy-nine years. If you divide these years into equal fifteen-year segments and link those segments to the times of a day, it looks something like this:*

0–15 DAWN,
16–30 MORNING UNTIL NOON,
31–45 MIDDAY,
46–60 AFTERNOON UNTIL TWILIGHT,
61–75 EVENING,
76+ NIGHTFALL.

'm a woman who is in full afternoon bloom, and I'm learning to love it. I admit that it hasn't always been this way for me, though. I recall the incredulous concern that accompanied the first hot flash and the tearful rending of my heart at long-waited-for graduations. I remember when it was that I learned to make enough food for only two. Some parts of this experience have been harder than others, and I understand that because you may be in the middle of one of those harder times, you might think that some of the humor I'll employ in what follows seems unsympathetic or unkind. Please don't misinterpret what I'm saying or the way I'm saying it. I've walked through some of these difficult times, and I'm looking back on them now, seeing them not only in their darkness, confusion, and despair but also in light and faith—and for me, that engenders humor. Perhaps you aren't able to laugh along now, but it also may be that a good laugh is just what you need. In any case, please don't feel misunderstood or unloved. The one whose love and understanding you need is there with you today, as he has always been, and he weeps and smiles with you.

It may also be that some of the chapters in this book won't apply directly to you. Perhaps you've never had children or worried terribly about those new wrinkles. I trust that the truths in each of these chapters will speak to your heart, however, even if it's only that you'll be able to help your sisters in their struggles. I don't mean to imply that women don't suffer through the throes of afternoon living if they don't have a husband, children, or grandchildren; these are the arenas where my blood has been spilled, and these are the fields that I've plowed.

Little Brown Traitors

Sitting here at my keyboard, as I have been doing a great deal of the time these past several years, my eye happens to land on my hands . . . and I'm reminded again.

It's been a lovely summer, and I've spent numerous delightful days at the beach, playing in the surf, laughing with friends. The blonde highlights in my hair have become more noticeable, and my freckles have been having a heyday, jumping up and screaming, "It's summer, and we're back! Let's have some fun!"

My hands have gotten browner too, but there's something else noticeable there, crowding out those friendly little harbingers of long days, salt spray, and warm sand. The tiny spots that used to pepper my skin pretty evenly are clumping together now in big brown blobs that remind me of my grandmother. My little freckly friends have turned on me and conspired to become age spots! Yes, it's true. No matter how I fight against it or try to ignore it, I'm getting older, and these superficial signposts aren't the only way that I can tell.

Habitat Alterations

In the last few years, my children have moved out . . . and so has my uterus, their first home. The grandchildren come for visits now, but they go home at the end of the day, and as happy as I am to see them come, I'm also exhausted when they go. *How did we used to do this?* my husband, Phil, and I wonder as we pick up the toys, groaning with each bend of the back and knee.

I have a new darling . . . my pillow. It has become my new best friend. When I can't be with my pillow, I dream about it, especially while I doze on the couch in the early evening, snoozing there because it's too early to go to bed. Phil and I watch the clock at night, yawning and waiting until we can finally lie down (9 P.M. is the Blissful Hour of Relief). Once we do finally acquiesce to our pillows' siren song, I find myself up at 3:30 A.M., reciting the books of the Bible and praying and wondering what happened to the days when I used to be able to sleep soundly through the night.

Standing in line behind my pillow is another new friend— I think he's Turkish. His name is Ottoman. I love that word— ottoman. *I just need to put my feet up for a little while* has become my newest mantra. Why don't they make Lazy Boy desk chairs and computers that hang from the ceiling so that I could be comfortable while I write? Ah, comfort, dear, sweet, comfort.

Senior Moments

We eat dinner at 4:30. When we go to a restaurant now, we're on time for the early bird senior special, and we're the youngest people there, or at least that's what we think. I've heard myself saying, "I can't eat late in the evening, because if I do, I'll be awake all night, taking antacid." When did I start saying that? What happened to the days when we used to be able to power down a double-double cheeseburger with fries and a chocolate shake at 10:15 P.M. without a second thought or a second taste?

Our eating has changed in other ways too, aside from the fact that we're usually done by 5:10 P.M. It's rather embarrassing but true: all sorts of funny things have been going on with my digestive system. The list of foods that I can't eat has been growing exponentially, and at a time when our culture is crying out for more and more tolerance, I've become progressively more intolerant. I carry Bean-O with me now, as well as Lactaid (what my family humorously calls Milk-O), because I've become lactose and all other yummy, healthy, filling-food intolerant.

I've become caffeine-intolerant too. I can remember a time when I could drink coffee all day and even at night and snicker at older women who said that they couldn't have it after noon or they would be awake all night. Now I'm the one who lies awake at 2:45 A.M. wondering what Starbucks demon possessed me to order just one little shot of espresso in the early hours of my day, so that I would have the energy to complete all my projects.

I've been asked if I want the senior discount at the movies by a smooth-faced, gum-chewing little nincompoop (I mean teenager) who wouldn't recognize a senior if his short, meaningless little life depended on it! (Just kidding!) Waitresses, now known gender-nonspecifically as servers, call me ma'am. Flight attendants (p.c. moniker for stewards and stewardesses) ask me if I want help putting my luggage in the overhead compartment. This summer a little four-year-old asked me if I was okay as I rolled around in the water by the shore. What was he thinking? Didn't I look okay? Wasn't it typical for a grandmother to take advantage of nature's free exfoliation and seaweed wrap?

Last year my husband received his invitation to join AARP in the mail. I thought that was hilarious until I got mine. *I'll show them,* I thought, as I tossed it into the trash.

Memories, Nothing More Than . . . Um, What Were We Talking About?

Speaking of the movies (we were speaking of the movies, weren't we?), I have a friend whose mother keeps a list of the movies she's seen because she can't remember if she's seen them or not. That used to strike me as humorous.

My children tell me stories that start out, "Remember when we . . . and then you . . ." and I say, "No, but I'm sure you're telling the truth. That sounds like fun. Did I enjoy myself?" My youngest son, Joel, and I were talking one day, and I asked him a question (about something, I can't recall just what now) and he answered, "Mom, the answer to that question is the same as it was an hour ago."

"Please tell me just one more time, and I promise I'll try to remember," I whined.

I'll admit that I was pretty skeptical about Hillary Clinton's inability to remember the facts surrounding the Whitewater land debacle, but now I'm not so sure. How old was she when she was subpoenaed to give testimony?

Sometime in the past, I'm not quite sure exactly when, my daughter, Jessica, remarked that every time she came over to my house I was ordering prescription drugs from my local drug store. Which reminds me . . .

I wear prescription glasses now and even have bifocal contacts. That's a relief, because I think I could have written another book in the time that I've wasted looking for my glasses during the last five years since I started wearing them.

I'm taller than my mother now—for the first time in my life—and I have the body of my paternal grandmother. I'm developing jowls and cellulite and wrinkles, and what's surprising is that I don't think I care anymore. My grandchildren love for me to snuggle them—I'm sure that I feel warm and squishy and soft and comfortable to them, just like she did to me. For some reason, even though I've spent years sweating at the gym, my eldest grandson, Wesley, hasn't yet bestowed the desired compliment, "Gee, Mimi, you're buff," and now I know that he probably never will. Oh well, where did that ottoman get to?

Well, you get the picture, don't you? I could go on and on (and I will) about the changes that women face in the afternoon of their lives. These decades are fraught with change, and just when we were finally getting comfortable with the way things are, everything is turned on its head. This book is about those changes, but that's not all that it's about.

A Comforting Meditation

The most comforting thought that I've been clinging to as I've experienced these changes over the last few years isn't a memory of those golden days of pleasure when my babies were little and my body was young. The sweetest comfort that I know comes to me in the form of a theological proposition: *God is my Father, he is sovereign, and he is good.* Throughout this book, I'll continually refer to the changes that we're going through as part of a sovereign Father's wise and loving plan, a plan in which God works out his ultimate design to glorify himself and change me into his image. Don't skip over that last sentence, because it's the key to joyfully embracing this, and every, time of life. God's supreme purpose in bringing me through all these changes is to glorify him and sanctify me.

We've all heard others speak of God glorifying himself, haven't we? I know that God is already glorious, but I also recognize that he seeks to glorify himself specifically through certain means in our lives.

What would God's glory look like in your life? It seems to me that God is glorified when I embrace this one joy above all others: *knowing him.* When my life shouts to everyone around me, *Knowing God is the best, most sweet, most satisfying aspect of life!* he's being glorified and exalted by me. When I face the ostensibly never-ending changes with grace and gladness, becoming like my valiant sister in Proverbs 31 who "smiles at the future" (Prov. 31:25), my family and friends know that God can be trusted, even though life is sometimes more like a uncertain roller coaster than a predictable merry-go-round.

How does the Lord create that kind of God-exalting praise in my heart? By teaching me that those facets of my life that I would tend to love and lean on (like a good memory, good eyesight, natural strength for the tasks at hand, or restful nights of sound sleep), can't support the weight of real life through eternity. They aren't the source of real joy, peace, or blessing. So, he removes familiar temporal joys, lovingly drawing my attention up to him, where I find fullness of joy and eternal pleasures (Ps. 16:11).

Romans 8:28–30 is a passage that most of us could quote. Paul wrote,

> And we know that God causes all things to work together for good to those who love God, to those who are called according to His purpose. For those whom He foreknew, He also predestined to become conformed to the image of His Son, so that He would be the firstborn among many brethren; and these whom He predestined, He also called; and these whom He called, He also justified; and these whom He justified, He also glorified.

Let's take Paul's teaching and paraphrase it with the present time in our lives in mind:

> *We can know and be assured that God causes everything you and I are going through, especially the painful changes in our bodies and our homes, to work profitably for our ultimate good; this is a good that will be enjoyed and embraced by those who love him and have*

adopted and adapted to his purpose in their lives. This good doesn't consist in the maintenance of the status quo or in the continuation of life as we have come to know and love it. Rather, it is worked out in our lives as we are remade, day by day, into the image of the Son, who said, "The foxes have holes and the birds of the air have nests, but the Son of Man has nowhere to lay His head" (Matt. 8:20); *and* "If anyone wishes to come after Me, he must deny himself, and take up his cross daily and follow Me. For whoever wishes to save his life will lose it, but whoever loses his life for My sake, he is the one who will save it. For what is a man profited if he gains the whole world, and loses or forfeits himself?" (Luke 9:23–25)

Just what is the Lord up to in our lives? Is he intrinsically involved in every change and has he mercifully arranged our lives so that we are forced to go through them? In the following pages, we'll examine how we experience some of those changes; we'll send up red flags when there's danger approaching; and we'll try to see, when we can, the lighter side. The truth is, though, that we don't need someone who will just sit and rock with us on the porch during these afternoon hours; instead we need help to envision them through the right bifocals—through God's plan, glory, and purpose.

Other valiant afternoon women are going to join in our discussion. You can find out more about them in the About the Contributors section at the back of this book. Each one of them is a friend of mine, and I've watched their lives as they've walked through the challenges of the afternoon years. I commend them and recommend that you drink deeply of their wisdom.

Are you ready to forge ahead into the unknown future? Are you smiling? Are you prepared to embrace all that God has laid in your path, knowing that his purpose and goals are good? If so, then let's pour ourselves a cup of tea (caffeine-free, herbal, if you please), put our feet up on good ol' Mr. Ottoman, and learn to appreciate the treasure that's being spread before us in this long afternoon journey.

one

To Everything There Is a Time

There is an appointed time for everything.
And there is a time for every event under heaven.
(Eccl. 3:1)

od's creation is filled with variation and dissimilarity. The ocean, the woods, the desert, the stars are each a different canvas for his handiwork. Gaze at a leaf and ponder the variety of his palette: emerald virescent leaves suffused with life fade into saffron, then transform into ochre vellum, swirling as they fall barrenly to the ground.

Have you ever wondered why leaves change? I don't mean to ask, "What are the scientific causes and effects that occur so that some trees are evergreens and others are deciduous?" I mean to ask whether you've ever pondered *Why?* What was God saying about himself to us when he created them to be that

21

way? What does this change teach us? "God made the two great lights, the greater light to govern the day, and the lesser light to govern the night; He made the stars also. God placed them in the expanse of the heavens to give light on the earth, and to govern the day and the night, and to separate the light from the darkness; and God saw that it was good" (Gen. 1:16-18).

Why did God divide the day into day and night? Why did he bestow two "great lights" upon us instead of only one? Why is the sun fiery and violent and the moon alabaster and bleak? Why does the sky transform from azure to tangerine in the evening or spend one day obscuring its elegance in shrouds of gray flannel only to joyously throw off its cloak in exuberant glory the next?

The Nature of Creation, the Nature of Creation's King

It seems to me that God loves change. In all of his creation there isn't anything that stays precisely static. In fact, even atoms are subject to variation, winding down as they are, seeking disorder rather than order. What in all creation doesn't change? Only God, the one who stands over the creation. Ponder with me his testimony about his consistent nature and our inconsistent world:

> Of old You founded the earth,
> And the heavens are the work of Your hands.
> Even they will perish, but You endure;
> And all of them will wear out like a garment;
> Like clothing You will change them and they will be
>   changed.
> But You are the same,
> And Your years will not come to an end.
>   (Ps. 102:25–27)

He who made the Pleiades and Orion
And changes deep darkness into morning,
Who also darkens day into night,
Who calls for the waters of the sea
And pours them out on the surface of the earth,
The LORD is His name. (Amos 5:8)

God sovereignly rules over all the day-to-day changes that we experience, and yet he never changes. "For I, the LORD, do not change," he states in Malachi 3:6. James speaks of this truth eloquently when he refers to God as "the Father of lights, with whom there is no variation or shifting shadow" (James 1:17). God reigns over the two great lights, the sun and the moon, but he stands above them. The moon phases in and out of fullness. The sun explodes violently in solar storms; its effect on us is lengthened and shortened as the earth turns on its axis through the seasons or is befogged by mist or gloom. But with God there is no "variation or shifting shadow."

> There is nothing of this kind with God; he is never affected by the changes and chances to which mortal things are exposed. He occupies no one place in the universe; he fills the heavens and the earth, is everywhere present, sees all, pervades all, and shines upon all.[1]

Why has the Lord so arranged the universe, from smallest molecule to the full course of our lives, so that we're constantly faced with change? Because he wants us to observe and to learn. To learn that we are finite, dependent, weak, in need of daily sustaining. And to learn that he's unlike us.

The Truth about Our Condition

About a year ago I noticed an odd bump on a joint of my ring finger. *What's that?* I wondered. I felt it and tried to move it about and fussed with it, all the while trying to ascertain what it was. Then, at a conference I was attending I spoke with a rheumatologist.

"What's this funny little bump thing on my finger?" I asked.

He took one moment to feel it and then said, "It's a Heberden node. Just part of aging; nothing more than a calcified spur of the joint cartilage."

"Ah, just a part of aging." Was that supposed to make me feel better?

The truth about our condition is that we're all aging—even though you may not have been graced with any funny little bumps yet. Not only are we aging, we're sprinting toward an eternity that will commence with a transformation that we can only guess about.

During my research for one of the chapters in *Women Helping Women,* I stumbled upon these astonishing sentences, "I am writing this book about death for an intensely personal reason. I have a terminal illness. You are invited to read it for the same reason. You too have a terminal illness. . . . Life is always fatal."[2]

Do you think much about this truth? Do you know that your life is winding down and that a day is hastening toward you with ever-increasing speed in which everything you know will be changed? All the illusions will be stripped away; all the falsehoods exposed; truth will become visible.

If you're like me, it's easy to forget these truths—until something happens that reminds us. My memory doesn't work, my children turn thirty, or I receive unwelcome news of a parent's illness, and the realities that used to dance around the corners of my consciousness are brought into focus, center stage. Life will not always be what it is today. I'm finite, I'm frail, I'm dependent.

Have you ever considered the recklessness of the young? I watch the young people in my neighborhood skateboarding and shake my head in wonder; they're young, and they feel invincible. They don't feel the ache and stiffness that is part of my morning, and the facts about the future seem no more real to them than that there'll come a day when skateboarding will no longer hold an allure. They take foolish risks because they don't know the truth that my little Heberden node has taught me: life is short, life is precious, and I'm vulnerable.

Finding Blessings in Little Bumps

Isn't God good? He could have left us without these changes and kept our ultimate fate from our eyes, until we would discover one day that everything had come to an end. Instead, he's set up signposts all along the way. Like the self-styled prophet on the street corner with his prognostication, "The End Is Near!" the Lord has placed within each of us a living handbill: "Think about what you're doing! Prepare for eternity!" The psalmist prayed that the Lord should "teach us to number our days, that we may present to You a heart of wisdom" (Ps. 90:12). It is interesting, isn't it, that it takes divine wisdom to know about the length of our days. John Calvin commented,

> Even he who is most skillful in arithmetic, and who can precisely and accurately understand and investi-

25

gate millions of millions, is nevertheless unable to count eighty years in his own life. . . . Men can measure all distances without themselves . . . they know how many feet the moon is distant from the center of the earth, what space there is between the different planets; and, in short, they can measure all the dimensions both of heaven and earth; while yet they cannot number seventy years in their own case.[3]

In several parables, Jesus lovingly warned us about the foolishness of not comprehending the brevity of life. In one he cautioned that we should always be dressed and ready for his return. In another, he warned the rich householder who was saying to himself, "I'm financially secure and can take my ease," that his soul would be required of him when he least expected it. The parable of the rich man who lived selfishly but later suffered torment while Lazarus basked in the pleasures he never knew also serves to teach the wise: Look at the Word! Observe the world! Read the headlines broadcast by the changes in your body!

The apostle Paul also admonished his readers, "Therefore be careful how you walk, not as unwise men but as wise, making the most of your time, because the days are evil. So then do not be foolish, but understand what the will of the Lord is" (Eph. 5:15–17).

Are you detecting a theme here? The truth about eternity and our fast approach toward it sifts the heart of each person. It reveals either a heart of foolishness or a heart of wisdom. Without the intervention of the Holy Spirit and because of the sacrifice of Christ, all that will ever be revealed about us will be foolishness. But with God's help, we can take to heart the notices he's placed along the way and become wise. How will we know this wisdom? It expresses itself in words like David's:

> "LORD, make me to know my end
> And what is the extent of my days;
> Let me know how transient I am.
> Behold, you have made my days as handbreadths,
> And my lifetime as nothing in Your sight;
> Surely every man at his best is a mere breath. Selah.
> Surely every man walks about as a phantom;
> Surely they make an uproar for nothing;
> He amasses riches and does not know who will gather
>   them.
> And now, Lord, for what do I wait?
> My hope is in You" (Ps. 39:4–7).

This heart of wisdom that we're after embraces several important facts.

You and I need God's help to gain the wisdom that Jesus, Paul, and David speak of. There is a deficiency in our understanding: not just a lack of knowledge but a willful reluctance to grasp the true state of our affairs. We need him to humble our hearts and cause us to be willing to love the truth.

There will be an end to our days here on earth. Even the most foolish among us give that truth tacit recognition. *Yes, yes,* we think, *I know my life will end someday . . . but just not this day.* This kind of foolishness is played out in hundreds of ways in our everyday lives. Do you need an example? Do you have a will? Seventy percent of us don't.

The life that we're now living is fleeting—at best it's a mere breath. The Holy Spirit inspired James, who called it a "vapor that appears for a little while and then vanishes away."

27

The next time you're getting out of the shower, look at the mirror. Then open a window and watch the fog clear away and ask God to grant you wisdom. Think, *That's what the length of my days is like.*

All the trappings of the world about which I am presently exercised are futility. Think about the last time that you were upset, angry, or worried. How important would these problems appear in heaven? Will it really matter if the paint on your dining room wall is too yellow or the certificates of deposit fell one-quarter of a point? As Mother Teresa said, "From heaven, the most miserable life on earth will look like one bad night in an inconvenient motel."[4]

Only our relationship with our heavenly Father through Christ will last. The truths about the impermanence of our lives and present relationships would cause us to despair if there were not one relationship that will endure through all time. In fact, our relationship with God through Christ was in existence in the Father's heart even before we were born, even before the foundation of the world (Eph. 1:4), and it's that relationship that will continue throughout all time.

This Is My Home . . . but Not Really

I love parties. For the last two years, I've tried to see how many people I can cram into my house (and spilling out the front and back doors) on Labor Day. This year we set up an Astro-Jump and kiddie pool in the front yard and pools in the back yard. We told the parents to furnish their children with water pistols. Adults and children were running amok through the house—some adults even got into a water fight with the hose! Can you believe it?

On at least two occasions during the day women came to me and said, "Why do you do this? Aren't you afraid your house will get messed up?"

"Ah," I replied, "it doesn't really matter, does it? It's all going to burn anyway."

This story may sound spiritual and noble. I did mean what I said at the time, but the following day, when I discovered that one of my picture frames in my office had been broken, I had a different view. It is true that this is all going to go away (2 Peter 3:10–12) and that my house, as nice as it is, isn't my home, but living that out when my picture frame is messed up is something different.

Just like everyone else, I have a tendency to love my things. You know what kind of things I'm talking about: my house, my car, my clothes, my books . . . my stuff. I love them, and though I might know the wise way to think about them, I have to struggle with putting off foolishness and putting on wisdom.

It's so easy to think that my little nest here is really what life is all about. My kids, my grandkids, vacations on the lake, soccer games, baby showers, grocery shopping: it's all so familiar and oh, so comfortable.

Aliens and Sojourners

One point of the changes that you're enduring is that you'll learn about Abraham's faith. Reflect on the words that describe his journey, "By faith Abraham . . . obeyed . . . ; and he went out, not knowing where he was going. . . . He lived as an alien in the land of promise, dwelling in tents . . . ; for he was looking for the city whose architect and builder is God" (Heb. 11:8–10).

Are you looking for *that* city? Are you seeking a "better country, that is, a heavenly one" (Heb. 11:16)? God has been kind to us by force-feeding us with change: change of home, change of job, change of family situation. He's been kind in that he's reminding us that this really isn't our home, that we're supposed to be looking for a different one. Think about these questions as you ponder his admonition, "Don't store up your treasure anywhere but in heaven."

Is your treasure in your home? Your Savior warns against the foolishness that would store up valuables in a place that is susceptible to damage. Do you know that it will all burn? Have you been able to appreciate what you have without investing your heart in it? How do you feel when something gets broken, stolen, or lost? It's right to be a good steward, but it isn't right to be a good idolater.

Is your treasure in your family? You are to love your family and cherish the time that God may be allowing you, but you're not to build your existence around them. Your existence is to be built on God, his kingdom, his righteousness. That way, when the kids go off to college and start a new life, your heart will be protected in heaven, where it belongs. If you're married, your husband is probably your closest earthly friend. You've been called to be a companion and helper to him, but you've not been called to make him your god. What would happen to your faith if the Lord took him home or if he fell into sin and left you? Is your heart safe with your Savior?

Is your treasure in your beauty? How do you feel when you see a new laugh line? Will life be worth living when you look like your grandmother? If you've spent your life trying to look good, then you'll be tempted to invest more and more time and money into your appearance in order to counteract the ravages of gravity, time, and our environment. I'm not saying that you shouldn't try to look acceptable, but the porcelain vase that's your face is too fragile to bear the weight of your heart.

Is your treasure in your health? What might the Lord teach you through feet that ache and hands that puff up like doughnuts? Would you be willing to serve him if to do so was uncomfortable, even painful? Again, I'm not saying that you shouldn't try to be as healthy as you can for as long as you can. I'm saying that no matter how many trips to the gym you make, how many reps you can do with free weights, and how many vitamins, minerals, and supplements you consume, you're getting older. God is freeing you from the pride and foolishness that the seemingly invincible youth embrace. The clock is ticking—live wisely!

He's the Director and the Playwright

Here's one more thought about why God loves for us to go through these changes: *His glory is so great that it is impossible for it to be displayed in a one-act play.* We might prefer for our lives to continue on, repeating the same pleasant scenes over and over, but he's interested in displaying his glory. He wants us to see how glorious he is in our youth—full of strength, wonder, energy. He desires that we learn how he is known in the years of our early adulthood—years filled with excitement, challenge, and new vistas. He wants us to learn what it means to be faithful a long time in one direction and how wisdom is more desirable than beauty, strength, or wealth. These are lessons about his perfections that we'll never learn until we've walked through them.

Take heart, dear sister. The changes that we're experiencing, although uncomfortable at times, are weaving a beautiful tapestry. This tapestry isn't about our beauty or how we've become so wise and wonderful. They're about his beauty and the excellence of his eternal plan. Instead of fleeing at breakneck speed in the opposite direction, why don't you take time now to look deeply into his design for you during these years, and pray, *Teach me, dear Lord, to number the days that I have left. I long to present to you and for your glory a heart that's filled with the wisdom that longs for heaven, that holds lovingly but loosely those you've gifted me with here, and that helps other women long to enter your kingdom and work, while we may, in your fields with joy.*

1. What are the changes you're going through right now? You can break them up into categories such as Changes in Myself; Changes in My Home; Changes in My Future.

2. What are the joys that are particularly attendant to the time of life that you're in?

3. What would "presenting a heart of wisdom" look like in each of these areas?

4. What have you already learned because of the changes you've experienced?

5. Read Deuteronomy 32:29, Ecclesiastes 9:10, and John 9:4. What do these verses teach us about wisdom? What changes do you think you need to make to begin to make better use of the time you have left?

6. Write out Ecclesiastes 3:1–8. What wisdom can you draw from these verses? Counselor and author Jay Adams writes about these verses: "The[se] examples show the utter undependability of anything (other than the process of change itself) in the present world. When Solomon speaks of every course of events being *appropriate for their time*, he is thinking of how appropriately God (not man) brings about the changes (or need for them) as He providentially changes the course of history. This plainly implies that we should not cling too tightly to things in the here and now."[5]

7. Summarize what you've learned in this chapter in three or four sentences.

two

The Valiant Afternoon Woman

Strength and dignity are her clothing,
and she smiles at the future. (Prov. 31:25)

can recall a vacation our family took when I was only four to the Sequoia National Park in California. Even after all these years, I still have in my mind's eye a memory of a tree that was so large at its base that a tunnel was made in it that a car could drive through. In that pristine forest grow some of the oldest life forms on earth; in fact, this grove of sequoias is several thousand years old. Think of it—when our Lord was walking through the deserts of Palestine, these evergreens had already been living for hundreds of years—and still they live on! Their longevity is due to their created nature: they are enormously strong and resistant to many of the parasites and diseases that plague other trees. On and on they grow—standing majestically with branches that stretch hundreds of feet into the heavens and roots that dig deep into the earth, deriving from it the sustenance they need.

As women, our life span is dwarfed by the evergreen's resilience. We usually have only seventy-five or eighty years on this earth, even if God blesses us with good health. The giant sequoias, by contrast, stand as hallmarks of endurance, adaptability, and august nobility. These magnificent trees not only instruct but also amaze us.

Majestic Women of Valor

In this chapter, I'm going to spend some time revisiting Proverbs 31. This is a passage of Scripture that's familiar to most Christian women, and one that encourages and convicts me. First, though, let's take time to read the passage. I've copied it in its entirety so that you can refer to it while you read this chapter. In light of the fact that it's so easy to skim over passages that are familiar, let me encourage you to stop and pray before you read it, asking the Lord to open your eyes to the fresh truth that it proclaims. The translation below is one that Hebrew scholar Bruce K. Waltke developed.[1]

> [10]A valiant wife who can find?
>> Her price is far beyond rubies.
> [11]The heart of her husband trusts in her,
>> and he will have no lack of "spoil."
> [12]She does him good, and not evil,
>> all the days of her life.
> [13]She selects wool and flax,
>> and works with glad palms.
> [14]She is like trading vessels—
>> she brings her food from afar.

¹⁵and she arises [like a lioness] while it is still night
and provides "prey" for her household
and the quota [of food] for her servant girls.
¹⁶She considers a field and purchases it;
with the fruit of her palms she plants a vineyard.
¹⁷She girds her loins with strength;
she strengthens her arms for the task.
¹⁸She perceives that her trading is good;
Her lamp [of prosperity] does not go out at night.
¹⁹Her hands hold out to the doubling-spindle,
Her palms grasp the spindle.
²⁰Her palm she spreads out to the poor
and she holds out her hands to the needy.
²¹She is not afraid for her household on account of
the snow;
for all her household is clothed in scarlet.
²²Coverlets she makes for herself;
her clothing is fine linen and [wool dyed with]
purple.
²³Her husband is respected at the city gate
when he sits with the elders of the land.
²⁴Garments she makes and sells [them];
sashes she supplies to the merchants.
²⁵Strength and majesty are her clothing,
and so she laughs at the coming days.
²⁶Her mouth she opens with wisdom,
and loving teaching is on her tongue;
²⁷one who watches over the affairs of her household,
the food of idleness she does not eat.
²⁸Her sons arise and pronounce her blessed;
her husband [also], and praises her:

29"Many daughters do valiantly,
> but you 'ascend above' all of them."
30Charm is deceitful, and beauty is fleeting,
> as for a woman who fears the Lord, she should
> be praised.
31Extol her for the fruit of her hands,
> and let her works praise her in the gates.
> (Prov. 31:10–31)

How does that passage of Scripture strike you? For many women, including myself, phrases like "she becomes like trading vessels" and "she arises [like a lioness] while it is still night" are fairly intimidating. How are we supposed to relate to this woman? Is she the original Superwoman? When I read this passage I'm tempted to ignore her or try to explain her away as some sort of ancient anomaly or idealistic analogy. I'd like to think that she's not a real person, just a personification of wisdom, or perhaps she's some man's idea of what he wishes his wife were like. *What am I supposed to do with her?* I wonder.

At times like this, when I'm wrestling with a particularly difficult passage of Scripture that seems, in some ways, foreign and impractical to me, I recall 2 Timothy 3:16–17. In this passage Paul is encouraging Timothy to recollect the beneficent power of the Word of God. He writes, "All Scripture is inspired by God and profitable for teaching, for reproof, for correction, for training in righteousness; so that the man of God may be adequate, equipped for every good work."

In light of this verse and others like it,[2] I need to remind myself that because this passage is God's Word, it's profitable and beneficial. There is something here that I need, and my heavenly Father, who is committed to preserving my soul and who is all-wise, has spoken it to me, whether I can wrap my mind around it at first or not. The Holy Spirit, through the apostle Paul, tells me that a right understanding and application of these words can teach, reprove, correct, train, and equip me. They will sustain me and help me grow strong.

Biblical Femininity Isn't Weakness[3]

It would be hard to miss how loudly this passage speaks about strength, competence, activity, and intelligence. The woman of valor isn't sitting at home popping bon bons, watching television, idly waiting for her husband to oversee or accomplish everything for her. No, she's involved in her own cottage industry, industrious in her home, and engaged in her community. She's concerned with the needs of the poor, but at the same time she doesn't fail to supply what her husband, children, and servants need.

This passage begins with the phrase "a valiant wife," and ends in verse 29 with the statement, "Many daughters do valiantly, but you 'ascend above' all of them." These two verses act like bookends to this song, and everything in between gives credence to the writer's fitting assessment of her. She's valiant and does valiantly! But what does it mean to be a valiant woman? What does this word tell me about how God evaluates the lives of women and of our lives particularly?

The Hebrew translated "valiant" and "valiantly," *hayil*, is primarily a military term meaning "strength, efficiency, wealth, army."[4] It is translated "army" eighty-two times, "strength" and "strong" ten times, and "valiant" or one of its cognates sixty-nine times in the Old Testament. It's obvious that King Lemuel's mother, the original author of these proverbs, wasn't using the word *hayil* to mean excellent or first rate, the way that this word is usually translated. An excellent wife was a woman of valor; she was courageous, bold, invincible . . . in a word, valiant! "The translators of the King James Version [who translated this adjective "virtuous"] were . . . sensitive to the heroic temper of the poem; their 'virtuous woman' in fact meant as much as 'heroic woman' in the English of that time."[5]

Throughout this passage, the valiant woman is painted in military pictures. These images do seem to fly in the face of our modern notions of femininity, which is possibly why some writers seem to want to allegorize her.[6] For instance, it's unusual to hear that a woman "girds her loins with strength; she strengthens her arms for the task," which is the literal translation of verse 17. In fact, "girds her loins" is a "masculine image, referring to an 'act that prepares one for heroic or difficult action, often for warfare.' "[7] Instead of speaking of her clothing as luxurious gold brocade or flimsy chiffon, her attire is described as "strength and majesty" in verse 25.[8] Again, the terms used are masculine nouns: "*strength* is a condition in which one can exert great force or withstand great force" (like the mighty sequoias) and *majesty* is used to describe "what is beautiful and instills awe and ascribing high value or status."[9] But the military imagery doesn't end there. She "laughs [in victory]," as over her enemies (Prov. 31:25), and she acts as a watchman or spy as she "looks well to the ways of her household" (Prov. 31:27 ESV).[10]

Revealing Lyrics and Dancing Feet

I recently had the opportunity to see the musical *Forty-Second Street* on Broadway. Although I was entertained by the upbeat singing and energetic dancing, I was troubled by the lyrics of one of the songs, "Keep Young and Beautiful." The lyrics in question, "Keep young and beautiful, if you want to be loved . . . Don't fail to do your stuff with a little powder and puff, Keep young and beautiful if you want to be loved,"[11] unmasks one philosophy at the heart of our society: If you want love, you'd better look pretty!

My auto-response to these lyrics was, *Excuse me?* Would it have been the same for you? Although our culture isn't usually quite so blatant in its superficiality, this is the truth that underlies and impels our fashion and cosmetic industry. "Don't look old! Don't look plain! Do you want to be loved?" These are the mantras that our civilization screams at us, but they aren't what the Bible teaches. We're going to take a closer look at beauty and aging in chapter 10, so I'll leave this topic with some wisdom from our valorous woman's song, "Charm is deceitful and beauty is fleeting, as for a woman who fears the Lord, she should be praised." This proverb stands in stark contrast to the idealized portraits of a woman whose beauty and charms allure and entice and are the ultimate measure of her worth.

What can we learn about how to live from this valiant woman? What are the characteristics of her life? As we face the afternoon of our lives, what qualities should we be focusing on?

She's trustworthy. Don't miss the importance of the statement, "The heart of her husband trusts in her" (Prov. 31:11). Typically the Bible warns us against trusting in people, as in Psalm 118:8, "It is better to take refuge in the LORD than to trust in man" (see also Ps. 62:8–9; Jer. 17:5–6; Micah 7:5; Ps. 118:9), but here King Lemuel extols her dependability and encourages her husband to lean heavily upon her.

She's benevolent. Consider the ways that she benefits others:

Her husband prospers because of her (Prov. 31:11).

She protects him from harm and actively seeks to bless him (Prov. 31:12).

She provisions her household (Prov. 31:14–15).

She cares for the poor and needy (Prov. 31:20).

She protects her household (Prov. 31:21).

Her words bring light, peace, and joy to others (Prov. 31:26).

Like a watchman on a tower, she watches over her household, ready to defend what God has entrusted to her (Prov. 31:27).

She's amazingly industrious! She works in the home and in the marketplace. In her home she works with "willing hands" (Prov. 31:13, 19, 22); she makes linen garments and sells them (Prov. 31:24). With her profits she buys real estate that she plants with "the fruit of her hands" (Prov. 31:16 ESV) as she continues to invest her money in profitable enterprises for her family's benefit. Her activity stands in stark contrast to other ancient literature that might forego seeing women as sex objects but fails to see them as anything more than inertly wise. She's not idle, sitting around pondering the truths of the universe, nor is she a nymphet, finding her value in sexual prowess. Her wisdom bursts forth in productive enterprise!

She is a woman who fears the Lord. The point of all this industriousness, oversight, and valor is not that she would be able to have more material goods or a more comfortable lifestyle for herself, or even that people will write poetry or sing songs to praise her. The point of everything she does is the pleasure of the Lord. She works hard, she sacrifices, she focuses on one goal: glorifying God. And her family is blessed because of it.

How Does She Reprove Us?

Looking over that daunting list, the numerous reproofs that she brings me are too obvious to say, so I'll focus on only one facet: *The fear of the Lord.* The mainstay of this valiant woman's life is the "fear of the Lord," while I find myself fearing almost anything but. I fear what will happen when my husband retires and what will happen to our children and grandchildren when they face these uncertain times. I fear another wrinkle, another pound of cellulite, another gray hair, loss of meaning, and ever-diminishing strength.

In addition to all these fears, I tend to compartmentalize my life, so that my day-to-day responsibilities are distinct or seemingly less meaningful than my other, more "religious" duties. So the valiant woman challenges me on two fronts: to see my entire life as consecrated to the Lord, from the mundane task of grocery shopping to the difficulties of book writing, and to grow in my fear of him. Since I recognize the ease with which we talk in Christianese, all the while missing the reality behind our familiar phrases, let's take one moment to look at what the fear of the Lord is.

Dr. Edward T. Welch writes that the fear of the Lord is "reverent submission that leads to obedience, and it is interchangeable with 'worship,' 'rely on,' 'trust' and 'hope in.' "[12] If the goal of my life is a fleshed-out acquaintance and worship that eventuates in submission and obedience to the King of my heart, then I won't find myself being unreliable, idle, self-centered, selfish, critical, self-indulgent, apprehensive, or vain. The driving motive of my life as I age won't be to try to look young or develop outward beauty. Rather, it will be to live out a love that has captivated my soul and made life worth living.

As you face these difficult decades, how does the woman of valor and her life reprove you? Here are some questions to ponder: What is the most pressing fear in your life? What terrifies you? What makes you stay awake at night with worry? Is it,

- your husband's future?
- your health?
- your children's or grandchildren's future?
- your finances?
- your value as a woman, as you age and your beauty transforms from that of a young, green sapling to a beautiful, strong sequoia?

The Valiant Woman's Correction

The life of the valiant woman serves not only as an example that shows me where I've erred, but also it shows me the right way to live. The valiant woman testifies that the purpose of my life is not me or personal gain but faithful service to those whom the Lord has given me to steward. As I age, I want to become known as a woman who is increasingly more trustworthy and dependable, more and more committed to working the vineyard God has given me. Rather than looking at these years as the time of our lives in which we can begin to slack off, the woman of valor teaches us to become more and more faithful and committed. And now that my children have moved out and I seem to have more discretionary time, these years present a perfect opportunity to become more like her.

In this book we'll try to see all the ways that we can change our perspective and grow in strength and dignity. We'll learn to be thankful for the time that we now have: time to work harder than ever for the good of those around us and to grow in the fear of the Lord.

"In sum, the valiant wife is an energetic, strong, charitable, competent and skilled entrepreneur and manager. [She] is a selfless breadwinner for the family and an important contributor to society. . . . She empowers her wise husband to lead the land in righteousness and justice."[13]

She's Ageless but She's Not Young

As we contemplate our valiant sister, one more thing is for sure: *she's not young*. Like the giant sequoia, her life experience and her reputation haven't been put together on a weekend makeover. Her branches reach into the courts of heaven, and her roots have plunged deep into the richness of the earth God has created. This is a woman who's lived life in the trenches, a woman who has known God, who has believed and wrestled and labored and wept and laughed for joy. She's the biblical paradigm of godly beauty and worth—and you can bet that she's got wrinkles born from late-night watches and more than few gray hairs that grace her face and testify of her worth.

She's the "woman with the issue of blood" (Matt. 9:20) who knew that the Lord was the answer to her problem and pressed in past the shortsighted, overly protective disciples. She's Lydia, the entrepreneur who heard a message that revolutionized her and her family's lives. She's Deborah, a sequoia of a woman who stepped up to fight for the glory of the God of Israel. She's Rahab and the woman at the well, whose lives sing to us of transforming grace and forgiveness. And she's Phoebe, the deacon and patron of the church, upon whom the great apostle Paul relied. These women were valiant and strong like mighty sequoias, and though they are dead, their lives continue to speak to us. So let's start now to put aside the false

45

and futile thinking of the world and ask the Lord to embolden and encourage us.

Who makes the sequoias so strong? Their Creator God. Who will make us strong? The Lord alone. As we learn to know, respect, and honor him, to obey and delight in his way, to trust and rest in him, we'll grow strong and resistant to all the diseases that attack our sisters, like fear of the future and futility. We'll find great nourishment and strength as we drink in broad drafts of heavenly water and imbibe rich nutrients from his character, all the while furnishing shade and comfort to those who have taken up residence in our strong limbs.

1. Read Proverbs 31:10–31. Write out below any phrases that are particularly meaningful to you. Why do they speak to you? Do they teach, reprove, correct, or train you? How so?

2. What do the magnificent sequoias teach you about being a woman of valor? Have you ever visited a forest and thought about how your life resembles these beautiful trees? What did your observance of this part of the creation teach you? How does it encourage you?

3. What have you learned about biblical femininity from this study? Have you ever thought of yourself as being a valiant woman? Read Psalm 18:31–39, in which you'll find much of the same military imagery. Do you believe that the dynamic power and transforming might of the Holy Spirit can make these verses true of you? Why or why not?

4. Like the American redwoods and sequoias, the cedar tree was highly valued in the ancient Near East for its strength and resistance to rot. What do the following verses, many of them about the cedar, teach you about growth, fruitfulness, and stability? How is this strength cultivated?

> How blessed is the man who does not walk in the counsel
>   of the wicked,
> Nor stand in the path of sinners,
> Nor sit in the seat of scoffers!
> But his delight is in the law of the LORD,
> And in His law he meditates day and night.
> He will be like a tree firmly planted by streams of water,
> Which yields its fruit in its season
> And its leaf does not wither;
> And in whatever he does, he prospers. (Ps. 1:1–3)

The righteous man will flourish like the palm tree,
He will grow like a cedar in Lebanon.
Planted in the house of the LORD,
They will flourish in the courts of our God.
They will still yield fruit in old age;
They shall be full of sap and very green,
To declare that the LORD is upright;
He is my rock, and there is no unrighteousness in Him.
    (Ps. 92:12–15)

The righteous will see and fear,
And will laugh at him, saying,
"Behold, the man who would not make God his refuge,
But trusted in the abundance of his riches
And was strong in his evil desire."

But as for me, I am like a green olive tree in the house of God;
I trust in the lovingkindness of God forever and ever.
I will give You thanks forever, because You have done it
And I will wait on Your name, for it is good, in the presence
    of Your godly ones. (Ps. 52:6–8)

The trees of the LORD drink their fill,
The cedars of Lebanon which He planted,
Where the birds build their nests,
And the stork, whose home is the fir trees. (Ps. 104:16–17)

Blessed is the man who trusts in the LORD
And whose trust is the LORD.
For he will be like a tree planted by the water,
That extends its roots by a stream
And will not fear when the heat comes;
But its leaves will be green,
And it will not be anxious in a year of drought
Nor cease to yield fruit. (Jer. 17:7–8)

5. Summarize what you've learned in this chapter in three or
   four sentences.

three

Just the Two of Us

It is not good for the man to be alone. (Gen. 2:18)

During a recent couples' meeting at our church, Phil and I were reminded about what life used to be like.

"We never have a date night," one woman complained.

"It's true," her husband confessed. "We just don't seem to have the time."

Several other couples in the group offered suggestions about how to carve time out of hectic schedules to be alone together. They suggested strategies about how to communicate deeply, enjoy each other's company, and remember what their marriage was all about.

Later, during a walk Phil and I were taking, I said, "Date night. What a concept, eh?" To which Phil remarked with wit, "For us, every night is date night." We chuckled as we walked along, remembering how harried life used to be, when the kids were home and we had to schedule time just to see each other. But our youngest son, Joel, moved out several years ago, and we're free to spend all evening talking to each other . . . if we're so inclined.

So, Now What?

You would think that our time of life would mark the renewal of relationship, wouldn't you? But, the statistics show that isn't the case. In fact, the highest incidence of divorce occurs among people ages forty to fifty-four. Not only do the statistics bear out that these years can be very trying, but it's women who are initiating and maintaining the single life. After the last child moves out, about 40 percent of the people who contact a divorce lawyer are women. Among divorced couples between the ages of 45–54, it is women who are choosing to stay single more than men. Do these statistics surprise you? After all those years together, it doesn't seem to make much sense to throw in the towel, or does it?

These data confirm what many women already know: Many a wife has spent her life focused on raising children, without ever being intentional about her relationship with her husband. Then, on that long-anticipated day when the mortarboards are finally thrown in celebration into the air, it seems as though much of the significance and meaning of the marriage has been suddenly and irretrievably discarded as well.

As a wife, you may have found yourself in a similar situation. As you sit, staring across the dinner table at your spouse, perhaps you've begun to wonder, "Well, now what? What topic of conversation should we attempt?" And, more revealingly, we wonder, "Why bother?"

The Genesis of Joyful Companionship

Imagine for a moment what it must have been like to wake up in the Garden of Eden, as Adam did so many years ago. Gradually, as he became aware of surroundings, ravishing sensations leapt into consciousness. He saw colors for the first time—hues so vivid, so alive—blues, greens, golds, purples, colors like we've never seen. What was the view he beheld from that mountain? How far could he see, with eyes that had never been tainted by sin, with a mind alive to perceive and understand what he saw? His heart must have been filled with great wonder and joy.

How would Adam have described what he saw? What words would describe the hues of the sky above—would robin's egg or cerulean come close? What about the grass, the trees, the fruit? How would he have portrayed the water in the river that ran out of the garden? Perhaps he would have described it in the same way that John described his revelation of the second garden: "And in the Spirit he carried me away to a great, high mountain, and showed me the holy city. . . having the glory of God, its radiance like a most rare jewel, like a jasper, clear as crystal. . . . Then he showed me the river of the water of life, bright as crystal, flowing from the throne of God" (Rev. 21:10–11; 22:1 RSV).

What does bright water look like? On a recent vacation, Phil and I visited the Blue Grotto, a cave on the isle of Capri, off the coast of Naples, Italy. To enter into the cave, we had to board a small rowboat and then duck down as our guide waited for a wave that would escort us into the darkness of the cave. Then we saw the most amazing sight. The water positively glowed. In the darkness of the cave, sunlight reflected off the sandy ocean floor and shone up through the water as it shimmered the most delightful shade of turquoise. But Adam's river was even more glorious. It was shining, brilliant, bright like crystal that refracted glorious color in prismatic splendor. In the midst of all this glory, you would think that we would hear Adam's songs of praise for his beautiful home . . . but we don't. In fact, we don't hear anything from him until later, after God added his crowning creation.

A Deficient Paradise

Before the first marriage, when the full extent of Adam's experience with fellowship and communication had been limited to walks and talks with his Creator, into this garden of pristine goodness and transcendent perfection, God made an astonishing evaluation: "It is not good that the man should be alone; I will make him a helper fit for him" (Gen. 2:18, ESV).

In our English Bibles it is easy to miss the full impact of God's startling assessment of Adam's condition. In the Hebrew, however, it's evident: God was not only saying that Adam's aloneness was merely lacking something that might have made it better. He was saying that his aloneness was positively bad.[1] The situation was dark and needed remedy, but Adam was yet unaware, so God caused all of the animals to parade before him. Then, as Adam inspected each one and named it accordingly, he noticed something troubling: he didn't see anyone who was like him. This was the very awareness that the Lord God was awaiting, so he remedied the situation immediately. He caused Adam to fall into a deep sleep, and God created Eve: someone like Adam and yet different from him. What was Adam's response? He rejoiced! "This at last is bone of my bones and flesh of my flesh," he intoned; "she shall be called Woman, because she was taken out of Man" (Gen. 2:23, ESV).

Adam's song of praise captures his heart's pleasure. After looking over all of the animals God had created for his help and enjoyment, Eve was the only one who was like him. She was the only one who corresponded to him. She was the only one with whom he would fit together perfectly. She alone would provide the companionship and help he so desperately needed.

A Perfect Helper

What kind of help did he need? If Adam had merely wanted to rearrange the garden or prune the trees, he had animals that were not afraid of him that he could use. Eve was not given to Adam merely to help him with his chores. (After all, there were no socks to pick up and launder then, were there?) Adam needed something from Eve that no animal could give him. He needed soul companionship and partnership in fulfilling God's mandate to rule over the earth and subdue it. He needed someone who was very much like him (he would probably have thought that he needed another man), but God surprised him by creating someone who was like him in many ways, yet distinctive in others. She could communicate, think, and experience emotion. She could love him and worship their Creator with him. Like him, she could partner with him, and Adam could find in her the mirror of his image but also the distinctiveness of his design. She was beautiful in that she was like him, but she was also beautiful in that she was different.[2]

It is fitting that the first words we hear from Adam are words of praise, but don't you find it astonishing that they aren't words of praise for the garden, as beautiful as it was, or for the varied and amazing animals, as good, strong, and beautiful as they must have been? The first words of praise that we hear from Adam are for his wife, Eve. She who was created to answer

53

to his aloneness, she who was to image her husband and her Creator, she's the focus of his first recorded worship! "At last," he exclaims, "someone who is like me . . . but also delightfully different!" Adam was exuberant because he was no longer alone! The one problem he had faced in the midst of all God's bounty and beauty had been solved by his gracious God. He had someone to talk to, to share his thoughts, dreams, and life with; someone who would help him see what he was and how he was to fit into God's creation. And she who had been formed from him would become one with him again, in marriage. All was right now—the garden was very good, at last.

We have to recognize that their bliss didn't last. Without spending time delving into what led up to the fall and their transgression (you can read about it in Gen. 3), let's look for a moment at the judgment God pronounced on the first couple.

> To the woman He said, "I will greatly multiply your pain in childbirth, in pain you will bring forth children; yet your desire will be for your husband, and he will rule over you." Then to Adam He said, ". . . Cursed is the ground because of you; in toil you will eat of it all the days of your life. Both thorns and thistles it shall grow for you . . . By the sweat of your face you will eat bread, till you return to the ground, because from it you were taken; for you are dust, and to dust you shall return." (Gen. 3:16–19)

Adam and Eve's transgression resulted in painful and difficult labor, loss of unity, and a new, hurtful desire for independence. They realized that they were naked—they were ashamed before one another, and they hid. Sin shattered what had been very good, and only the remnants remained.

About now you might be saying, "Thanks for the history lesson, but what does this have to do with me, in my marriage today?" Would you be surprised if I said "Everything"? Since the fall, every married couple has had to fight against the propensity to live lives of a separate existence marked by concealment, independence, and mistrust. In place of the harmonious partnership focused on God's glory that Adam and Eve knew, our lives more closely resemble two ships passing in the night. God's pronouncement on Adam, "It isn't good for you to be alone," is still relevant to us—but now we have a harder time believing it.

How Long Have You Been Alone?

Even though statistics seem to speak otherwise, I don't think that marriages deteriorate just because we enter into our fourth decade. I think that this failure has been progressing for much longer, but only now do we finally have time to notice how silent the house has become. Being in the afternoon of life doesn't mystically cause a marriage to become a black comedy with a dreadful ending. This script has been playing out for some time. We've been too busy with soccer practice and science projects and birthday parties to notice the erosion that's been eating away at the foundations of our life together.

Think back to how life was before you had children. For some of us, those starts might have been rocky; for others they might have been quite lovely and peaceful. Stop now to ponder the following questions:

- What was it about my husband that I loved when we were first married?
- When did I last delight in being with him?

- What did we talk about before the children and the years crowded out meaningful communication?
- When did you last thank God for your husband and mean it?
- When did you look forward to spending time alone with him?

Caves of Benign Resignation

I love the passages in John's Gospel about Mary and the death and resurrection of her brother, Lazarus. You remember the story of Jesus visiting with these three singles, Mary, Martha, and Lazarus, and Mary spending time learning from Jesus. Defying accepted cultural norms, Jesus defends Mary's desire to sit at his feet rather than pull kitchen duty. Her heart is filled with faith and ardent love for her Master.

But some time after Jesus leaves Bethany, Lazarus falls ill. "He whom You love is sick," Mary writes to her Lord. You can hear her unsaid words, "Please come and help him." But then we read the most astonishing sentence, "So when He heard that he was sick, He then stayed two days longer in the place where He was" (John 11:6). And in the meantime, Lazarus died.

Can't you imagine Mary's bewilderment, disappointment, and despair? Can't you see her and Martha talking with one another, encouraging each other as Lazarus became more and more gravely ill?

"Don't worry," Mary might have said, "the Master will come."

"I've heard that he's only two days away.[3] If he hurries, he could help Lazarus."

And then Lazarus died. "Where is the Lord?" they undoubtedly wondered. "Why didn't he come?" As they prepared Lazarus's body, wrapping it in grave clothes and anointing it with precious ointment, grief and despair overwhelmed them. Jesus was their friend. He was a healer. He could have prevented this. But the reality was that four days had elapsed while all hope for relief seeped from their hearts, just as the life had flowed out of Lazarus's body.

If Only You Had Been Here

Although most of us don't know the agony of having a beloved younger brother die of illness, we all do know the despair of seeing portions of our dreams for our marriage lie dormant and cold. Perhaps there are parts of your marriage, expectations, or hope for your relationship with your husband that you haven't revisited lately, so let me help you probe your heart a little by asking you to think deeply about these questions.

- What part of your marriage is like Lazarus in that tomb?
- What dreams have you rolled a stone over so that you can keep the shame of failure away from the light of your disillusioned eyes?
- What part of your marriage have you stopped praying about, given up talking about, hoping for, anticipating?
- What hopes are too painful to even think about reviving?
- Do you see yourself as created to be your husband's helper? Have you become defensively independent and self-sufficient?
- What topics have become anathema to you because, now that you've finally developed a hardy callus over your disappointments, it would be too painful pull it away?

- What part of your heart is like Lazarus's tomb? Dark, lifeless, filled with the stench of regret and "if only"?

Perhaps you're not on the verge of a divorce, or perhaps you are, but if you recognize that there are segments of your heart where you've given in to what my friend Carol Cornish[4] calls "benign resignation," then you know what I'm talking about.

Please don't misunderstand. I'm not saying that you've given up on the Lord. I'm sure that Martha and Mary knew that Jesus could help if he wanted to. They both believed in the resurrection. The problem wasn't the orthodoxy of their faith. It was that their faith didn't extend far enough into their present heart-wrenching circumstances. It didn't penetrate into the obscurity of their disappointment, and they had figured out a way to live self-protective, albeit grieving, lives. I'm not saying that it's wrong to learn to live with disappointment. We all do. But we have to guard against covering our disappointments with a veneer of pretense that puts on a brave but anemic smile, while we grit our teeth and wallow in an "It's okay . . . really, I'm fine" variety of unbelief.

Now is the time to revisit those dark crannies of unbelief and despair and invite Christ to bring his resurrection power in. Perhaps you need to start praying for your husband as you've never prayed before. Perhaps now is the time for you to say that whether he ever changes or not, you're going to find the faith that says more than, "It's okay, really, I'm fine." You've got to believe for the faith that says, "These things are a good in my life. My heavenly Father is using this very circumstance for his glory and my good and so, although I would like my husband to change in certain areas, I can rejoice even when he doesn't. What was once a rotting body of unbelief has become a source of life, faith, and joy to me, because I see my Father's hand in it."

The presence of Jesus turns death to life, darkness to light, tragedy to blessing! He causes what once looked like a curse to become a source of joy. Perhaps your husband isn't now (and never has been?) what you'd hoped he'd be. Even so, God has promised that he will give you everything you need for life and godliness in the knowledge of him. The hard yet comforting truth is that God has given you the husband you need to teach you about God's character. He's chosen your husband for you so that God can fashion you into the helper he wants you to be. To what end? Do you remember what I wrote in the first chapter? *He's given you the husband you have for God's glory and your ultimate good.* So, in all the places where you feel that you are suffering or disappointed, you can yet rejoice that God has engineered this problem for purposes that extend beyond your immediate happiness—right into eternity.

Bringing His Light into Your Caverns of Hopelessness

Let me encourage you that, by God's grace, you can change, even if like me you've been married nearly thirty years. You can learn to rejoice in your disappointments, to see them as gifts from a loving Father, and you can bring his light into your present circumstances. Here are some steps that you can begin today:

- Pray for yourself, your unbelief, your caves of disillusionment and regret. Instead of passing over them or ignoring them, begin to pray again, asking God to bring joy to your heart.
- Confess your lack of faith and your "if onlys" to the Lord. Speak openly to the Lord and tell him of your

concerns. He didn't reprimand Lazarus's sisters for saying, "If only you had been here." You can come to him now and ask him to remake your desires so that they fit more closely with his. Now is the time to confess any unbelief that you may have about his ability to change either you or your husband or cause his kingdom to flourish because of your trial.

- Try to identify any self-focused manipulating that you use, such as coldness, quietness, pouting, or independent self-sufficiency, and begin today to put it off. Put on Christ-centered praise and thanksgiving.

- Pray for your husband and thank God for him. You can pray for his growth in holiness and Christ-likeness, but don't stop there. Pray also that God would enable you to begin to enjoy him for who he is and see the good that he is in your life.

- Don't nag him about areas of weakness in his life, but don't ignore them either. Seek to speak respectfully and humbly into his life, while you continue to hope for God-glorifying change in both your lives.

- Control your speech by avoiding slander or gossip about your husband. Ask the Lord to make you aware of patterns of complaining or faithless talk.

- Seek to rebuild bridges where they've fallen down. What would really say, "I love you!" to him? Why not make his favorite meal, turn off the television, light some candles, and tell him all over again how happy you are that the two of you have time together, at last! You might also do this by taking an interest in his areas of interest. For instance, if he's a golfer, try to learn something about the game or ask him if you can go with him and ride in the cart (if you're like me and couldn't hit the ball if your life depended on it!). What are his areas of expertise? What makes him tick?

- Look for opportunities to be together, and then use them to practice being a servant. Even the most hard-hearted husband won't be able to resist you if you're willing to follow in your Savior's footsteps and take up the basin and the towel. Will you wash his feet?

- Find a friend to be accountable to. I'm sure that you probably have a friend or two you could enlist as a helper for you—to ask you the tough questions, to pray for you, and to encourage you as you seek to revital-ize your marriage.

For His Sake

In 1 Corinthians 11:8–9, Paul makes the most astounding statement. He says, "Man does not originate from woman, but woman from man; for indeed man was not created for the woman's sake, but woman for the man's sake." Here's the truth about why you've been created and placed in the relationship you're in: It's for your husband's sake. He's the one the Lord looked at and determined, "It's not good for him to be alone," so he created a woman to fill that niche. Ultimately, everything we do is to be oriented around the Lord, for his glory and his kingdom, but the place where we've been called to do that is in this particular relationship with this particular man. As you pon-der these truths, may I encourage you to think deeply about how you can answer his aloneness and grow in wisdom as a fitting helper? Your Father knows what you need, and he can grant you grace to find great joy at this sometimes stormy time of life.

1. Read Genesis 2:15–25. What do you learn about the Garden of Eden, Adam's place in it, and the creation of Eve?

2. What do the truths you identified above have to do with the way you should live your life today?

3. Would your husband say that he's alone? I don't mean that he's alone because he's stranded on a desert island. Would he say that even though he's in the midst of a household filled with people, he's alone in his calling, his spiritual life, his heart? What could you do today to begin to be a companion to him? Why not start by asking him if he feels alone? If he normally shies away from intense conversation, let him know that you want to be a companion to him and that you're looking for ways to do that. You could ask him the following questions:

   > Do you ever feel like you're alone in the battles you face every day? What are those battles? How could I help you? How should I pray for you?

   > Do you sense that I am here for you, supporting and encouraging you? (Let him know that you want a real answer, not just the one that he thinks will make you happy—and then listen to his responses, without responding defensively.)

   > Is there anything you would like me to do to help you? What do I do that's helpful for you? Where can I grow?

   > Would it be all right for me to go with you when you play (golf, softball, cards, football . . . whatever), just so that we can spend some time together?

4. What are the caves of benign resignation that you've been able to identify? How are you responding to this truth? Read John 11. What does this narrative tell you about Christ's resurrection power? What would his invading presence look like in your cave of desperation? Do you believe that your cave of desperation can turn into a delightful blue grotto?

5. What good has come out of this disappointment? If it's hard for you to see it now, pray that the Lord would help you see the good that he's brought into your life and the lives of others through this.

6. What would "rejoicing in tribulation" look like in your life? Write a prayer of humble acceptance and reliance on God.

7. Summarize what you've learned in this chapter in three or four sentences.

four

Don't Forget
to Write

May the Lord watch between you and me when
we are absent one from the other. (Gen. 31:49)

Scrapbooking is all the rage these days, isn't it?
Because I do quite a bit of speaking to women's
groups and have the chance to attend women's
retreats fairly frequently, I'm aware of all the different crafts
that women love to do. And, at least in recent years, scrapbooking has been the craft of choice.

What does your scrapbook look like? I don't have one. I
mean, I have boxes of pictures that, as of about two years ago,
were organized and categorized. "Where's that box with the sun-
set pictures? What about the birthday party collection?" my son
Joel and I asked each other as we went through those envelopes
of developed photographs from previous years and previous lives.

For our twenty-fifth wedding anniversary, our children created a beautiful scrapbook for Phil and me. What a precious gift! Each one of them took certain sections and decorated the pages. The pictures are wonderful, but their personality and humor that positively jump off the page mean the most to us.

I treasure our anniversary book because it reminds me of the memories that I've been collecting over the last three decades. In some ways, these memories have defined my life, enriched my soul, inscribed the narrative of my existence across days that have fused together into sonorous portraits painted in tears, laughter, and joy.

What do I remember? What photographs have been indelibly etched into my heart? When I close my eyes and bring to mind the days that are even now fading in brilliance and color, I still see varied and vivid pictures of a life spent as Mom.

I see harried days that were filled with little smiles, halting attempts at mastering walking, and then speech. I see T-ball and snack shacks. I remember coercing Jessica, our daughter, to try out for softball (something we had to do every year) because she was so afraid that she would fail.

I recall the sweet perfume of baby shampoo wafting up from newly washed hair. I can relive the joyous giggles and squirming shrieks of mirth as we made funny noises blowing on a toddler's little belly. "Stop, stop!" they would scream. "Oh, you want us to stop? Okay," we would say, and then the minute they tried to get up we would grab them, and the giggling would start all over again. I remember wild "Slime" fights that stained our walls as we contended for family domination, and I remember Capture the Flag in the canyon by our house.

We had a lot of fun in our house, but it wasn't all fun. I remember their tears and my offense at their not receiving the coveted invitation to "that party." I recollect losing seasons that never seemed to end and spelling lists that escaped memory when test time came. I can still hear the slammed doors and how I had to control my temper as I reopened the door and told the child to close it again, please, nicely. I remember saying, "Ask forgiveness from your brother and give him a hug. Tell him you love him." I also remember hearing, "You always pick on me!" "You never see what he/she does wrong!" "This place is like a prison! Why can't you be like other kids' parents?" "Mom, why do you have to ruin every movie? You know, not every movie has a 'deeper meaning.' Sometimes, it's just entertainment!" There were days that I waited until Phil got home from work and uttered the dreaded words, "You've got to discipline *that* child again."

I remember reading The Chronicles of Narnia and going to the midnight showing of *The Empire Strikes Back*. I recall discussions about why the movie *Desperately Seeking Susan* and black eyeliner were inappropriate; why earrings (on the boys) and tattoos and piercings (on them all) wouldn't be their best choices. I remember long hair that needed washing (where did that baby shampoo go?) and blistered sunburns and loose teeth and tubing down the river and the chicken pox and poison ivy and buckets by the bed because it was flu season.

And I remember trying to explain why it's important to know what the Bill of Rights says and trying to hide my tears when I listened to Joel recite the Gettysburg Address.

I also have more recent memories. I remember their graduations from high school and college, and James's graduation from boot camp as company honorman, and I remember the days that two of the three of them were married.

These are the pictures in my scrapbook. They are living. They are my delight. They are the legacy to how Phil and I have lived for the past thirty years and most especially to God's merciful grace. What does your album say? What precious memories fill the pages of your mind? What are they worth to you?

Catch 22

At the parent orientation for our son Joel's college, I sat with an old friend, Annie, and her husband, Finn. Their daughter, Hannah, was starting school with our son, and we reminisced about our times as their parents.

"I don't get it," Annie said. "Why do they have to grow up and go away?"

It did seem hard to explain, I'll admit. It seemed that the more seriously we took God's injunctions to nurture and train our children, the more deeply we involved ourselves in their lives, the more it hurt when it was time to give them up. Why *did* they have to grow up and go away? Why couldn't we keep life as it was? We were caught in a difficult situation. The choices seemed limited to these two: Ignore God's commands to pour into our children and train them for his glory, spending our lives in building a life apart from them, or pour our hearts and souls into them and find ourselves alone at the end of the day. Some choice.

Life Is a Series of Divestitures

Some time ago, I heard a professor at a local seminary make an astonishing statement. He said, "Life is a series of divestitures."[1] Even though that chapel service has faded from memory, that statement has stuck with me over the past few years. Think about it: "Life is a series of divestitures." A divestiture is an unclothing, a stripping, a dispossessing;[2] it is a letting go, a dismantling.

Once our first grandchild, Wesley, started to crawl, it wasn't long until he was headed out our sliding glass doors to investigate the back patio. "Look, Jessica," I said. "He's already on his way out." "Mom!" she objected, "don't say that!" "It's important that you see this, take it into your heart, and treasure these times," I warned her. "They'll be over before you know it."

From the moment our children are born, they're headed out the door. And just think of it, we encourage them along the way! How terrible it would be to try to keep them in diapers, to stop them from exploring, growing, changing. But every time we encourage that forward progress, we're hastening the day, and properly so, when we will have to divest ourselves, unclothe ourselves from our mom's uniform, and put on a different costume instead.

Our lives with our children seem as if they'll never change. And sometimes we fight militantly against this change when we see it coming, trying to control and mother our dear fledglings long after the Lord has called us to let go. When did he grow such strong wings . . . must I really let her fly?

Have you experienced their absence yet? Have you been divested? Remember what we discovered in the first chapter: "To everything there is a season." What does this season look like for you? Changing clothes can be difficult, especially when those old jeans fit so nicely and we're not quite sure just yet what we'll be putting on in their place.

My husband wasn't the first father to let a child go. We learn about love and divestiture when we look at our heavenly Father. He was the one who sent his only begotten Son out from his glorious home in heaven to be born as an infant in a filthy cattle stall. He was the one who sent him to those who "would not receive him," even though they had been created by him. He's the Father who turned his back on his Son as the Son cried out in anguish, "Father, why have You forsaken Me?" And he's the one who expended his furious wrath upon his beloved Son for the sake of his elect. He knows all about divestiture. Consider what you're learning to share in of his character as you ponder these verses:

> "For God so loved the world, that He gave His only begotten Son, that whoever believes in Him shall not perish, but have eternal life." (John 3:16)

> "He who did not spare His own Son, but delivered Him over for us all, how will He not also with Him freely give us all things?" (Rom. 8:32)

> "By this the love of God was manifested in us, that God has sent His only begotten Son into the world so that we might live through Him. In this is love, not that we loved God, but that He loved us and sent His Son to be the propitiation for our sins. (1 John 4:9–10)

Not only did God lovingly and willingly give up his Son for our sake, but also the Son gave up his right to demand equality with God:

> Have this attitude in yourselves which was also in Christ Jesus, who, although He existed in the form of God, did not regard equality with God a thing to be grasped, but emptied Himself, taking the form of a bond-servant, and being made in the likeness of men.

Being found in appearance as a man, He humbled Himself by becoming obedient to the point of death, even death on a cross. (Phil. 2:5–8)

Your heavenly Father and your wonderful Savior know all about divestiture. They know what it means to love and to give up proximate relationship for the love of another. They've gone before you in this sacrifice, and you can count on them to give you the grace and strength that you need to find when your heart is aching. You can be sure that they are molding your character to be more and more like theirs.

Ephemeral Treasures

Consider also, that although our giving up of our children is difficult, they aren't ours to begin with. Only the Father and his Son owe their relationship and filial love to themselves. All of our love for our children is derived. We don't have first claim on our love for our kids, nor can we even say that they belong to us. They belong to God and are gifts from his hand, as the psalmist knew, "Behold, children are a gift of the Lord" (Ps. 127:3). Every breath they take from their first startled cry all the way to the end of their days—their entire life is a gift from his hand.

As their parents, we are only privileged managers or overseers of the precious lives God has entrusted to us. We forget that he has plans for our children that were decreed in eternity past, and we think that we've got to make everything happen in just the way that we think it should. So we nag and cajole and manipulate and worry. We're astonished when they go their own way, and we forget that we're just operating as their tutors: more loving, committed, or engaged than an after-school tutor, perhaps, but we're merely tutors nevertheless. We didn't give them life; we didn't bring them into the world; they weren't created for our glory. The truth is that we're only shadows or metaphors for the realities of a Father and Son who make everything else in their image and bring everything to themselves for their glory by the Holy Spirit.

> He is also head of the body, the church; and He is the beginning, the firstborn from the dead, so that He Himself will come to have first place in everything. For it was the Father's good pleasure for all the fullness to dwell in Him, and through Him to reconcile all things to Himself, having made peace through the blood of His cross. (Col. 1:18–20)

We weren't created to bring everything into subjection to ourselves, and our children weren't given to us to glorify us. They're God's, and the fact that they're now independent adults serves to remind us of these realities.

If Onlys and Do-Overs

There are certain words that seem to bring gloom with them whenever they're uttered. *Regret* is one of them. Regret is a "feeling of sorrow, repentance, [or] disappointment over an action or a loss."[3] One of the more troubling aspects about our empty nest is that all our opportunities to do better next time are over, at least with these children, and we're left with memories stained with tears of "If only I had . . ." and the desire to make things right. Our default position, "I'll do better tomorrow," loses relevance when they pack up their bags and we wave good-bye to them from the front door. "I won't lose my temper any longer" . . . "I'll pray with him about his friends" . . . "I'll spend time just talking about whatever she wants to talk about" . . . "I'll live as a transparent, bold, and loving witness for Christ" . . . Each of these assertions of a hopeful new tomorrow are, for the most part, over now.

Many women struggle with regret and its by-product, guilt. Why didn't I spend more time with him? Why didn't I love her more? Can't I have another opportunity to make this right? These are the questions that torment many women, and this is one of those precious places where the forgiveness of Christ and the trust in his sovereign rule are most comforting.

Let's think a little about the forgiveness that's ours in Christ and the comforting truths of God's sovereignty. What is your favorite verse on forgiveness? For most Christians, it's 1 John 1:9, "If we confess our sins, He is faithful and righteous to forgive us our sins and to cleanse us from all unrighteousness." Who is it that will forgive and cleanse us? First John 1:7 tells us, "The blood of Jesus His Son cleanses us from all sin." If you merely skimmed over these verses, please go back and reread them. Meditate on them; what are they saying to you? This is what they said to that prince of English preachers, Charles Spurgeon:

> If thou lookest up to where that blood is streaming from the hands and feet and side of Jesus; if thou dost trust thy broken spirit in his hands, there is pardon for thy crimson sins to be had just now. . . . Say unto Him, "Father, I have sinned." Bury your head in His bosom; receive His kiss of forgiveness, for God delighteth to pardon, and to blot out transgression. Now that he has smitten Christ, He will not smite any sinner who comes to Him through Christ. His wrath is gone, and He can

73

now say, "Fury is not in me." Here, then, is a great wonder . . . [here is the] precious truth that is, "The blood of Jesus Christ his Son cleanseth us from all sin." . . . Now we see, then, that, whatever your sins may have been, they are all included in those little words, "all sin"; therefore be of good comfort, poor sinner, if thou believest in Jesus Christ, thou art born of God, and his blood cleanseth thee from all sin.[4]

How precious are these thoughts to me! As I reflect back on all the if onlys, all the squandered opportunities, all the times when I said too much, didn't listen, retreated into sinful self-protection, thought that a clean house was more important than a humble heart, all I can cry is, "Lord, be merciful to me, the sinner!" Thank God for his indescribable gift to us in Christ!

Can you think of anything that you need to ask God to forgive you for? Here's a partial list of sins that I've found in my life and in the lives of other moms. See if they resonate with you. If they do, don't give up in self-condemnation—instead run to Jesus Christ, the Comforter of poor sinners like us!

Demandingness: demanding that my children do what I want them to do when and in the way I want them to do it, without regard to their particular strengths, weaknesses, or giftings.

Pride: believing and acting as though their successes and failures are due entirely to my parenting skills, without reference to their gifts and choices or God's gracious sovereign rule.

People-Pleasing: wanting my children to perform well in front of others so that they will approve of my mothering skills, rather than encouraging the children to focus their thoughts and obedience on Christ and delighting in his glory.

Resentment: believing and acting as though I ought to be rewarded by my children for my sacrifices, rather than seeing my service as a God-given opportunity to grow in Christlikeness and bear witness to his goodness.

Unforgiveness: bearing a grudge or rehearsing over and over my children's failures and sins, even if they have repented of them or sought to do better, forgetting Christ's gracious offer of forgiveness of my habitual sins.

Hypocrisy: demanding that my children obey and honor me in ways that I do not obey or honor the Lord; refusing to confess my sins against them but insisting that they do so to me.

Laziness, Impatience, and Unbelief: giving in to discouragement when I don't see the rapidity or degree of change that I want to see in my children; letting them do whatever they want.

Craving Their Friendship: desiring my children's approval and friendship more that I desire the friendship and approval of the Lord; letting my kids call the shots so that I don't offend them or anger them.

Self-Centeredness: believing and acting as though my children belong to me and were entrusted to me for my pleasure rather than for the Lord's.

Legalism: creating unbiblical standards of behavior for my children that are not clearly laid out in Scripture and then justifying my position by saying, "Because I told you so, and you have to honor me."

As I've read over that list, I can see myself in every example. Let me remind you again of Spurgeon's words, words that are sweet to my soul: "Now we see, then, that, whatever your sins may have been, they are all included in those little words, 'all sin'; therefore be of good comfort, poor sinner, if thou believest in Jesus Christ, thou art born of God, and his blood cleanseth thee from all sin."

But asking forgiveness from the Lord is frequently not the end of our obligation. If we've sinned against our children, then we also have an obligation and the privilege to ask for forgiveness from them as well. Ken Sande, director of Peacemaker Ministries, has developed the following Seven A's of Confession that would be helpful for you to consider as you think about confessing your sin to your children.

The Seven A's of Confession

(The Seven A's of Confession are based on Matthew 7:3–5; 1 John 1:8–9; and Proverbs 28:13)

1. Address everyone involved (all those whom you affected)
2. Avoid if, but, and maybe (don't try to excuse your wrongs)
3. Admit specifically (both attitudes and actions)
4. Acknowledge the hurt (express sorrow for hurting someone)
5. Accept the consequences (such as making restitution)
6. Alter your behavior (change your attitudes and actions)
7. Ask for forgiveness[5]

I can imagine that for some of you this might seem to be a daunting task. For some, your relationship with your children has been strained or possibly even nonexistent for years. The thought of contacting them, of confessing sin, fills your heart with fear. "What will they say?" "Will they think that everything we stood for was wrong?" "Will they lose respect for me?" "Will they still love me?" "How can I admit to them that I'm a sinner?" Let me encourage your heart with the following verse from Proverbs: "He who conceals his transgressions will not prosper, but he who confesses and forsakes them will find compassion" (Prov. 28:13).

At the end of this chapter, I've included a possible outline for a letter you might want to write to your children. Please don't let fear or pride steal this opportunity for you to find compassion. Once I believed that for my children to love and respect me, they had to think that I was perfect. Now I recognize that their love and respect will flow more easily to me as a woman who is flawed but growing in humility and love. Think about the promise in the verse above, "He who confesses and forsakes his transgressions will find compassion." I long for the compassion of the Lord and my family, and this verse gives me concrete instruction on how to obtain it.

While we're speaking of regrets, let me leave you with one more thought. Even if you have confessed your sins to the Lord and to your children, you might still be struggling with forgiving yourself. The Bible never directs or commands us to forgive ourselves. Whenever we're filled with self-loathing or thoughts of "I can't believe that I would do such a thing," we're denying the truth about our inherent sinfulness. Instead of saying, "I can't believe that I was that bad," we should be thinking, "I can't believe that I was that good," or "I'm blessed that God kept me from being even worse."

His Sovereign Rule

The Lord is ruling from his throne, as he has throughout all eternity. He gave us the children that we have, and he's ruling and overruling in their hearts according to his sovereign plan. The one truth that comforts my heart above all others is that God can use even my failures as a mother to form the character of Christ in my children! Of course, that doesn't mean that I should ignore my failures or encourage others to do so. It's just that failure is part of all of our lives, and God uses even this for his glory. Remember, it wasn't only the good kings in the Old Testament who had good sons! Amon was one of the wickedest kings in all of Israel's history, and yet his son, Josiah, was one of the finest. God rules sovereignly over our lives and the lives of our children. And in this precious truth we can find true rest.

Even if your children live close by and even if you have a delightful relationship with them, the change from chief cook and bottlewasher can be trying at times. Let me encourage you to think again about God's goodness to you in this season of your life. Why not thank him that he's allowed you to come this far and seek to rejoice in the blessings that you have?

1. What are the most precious pictures you have in the scrapbook of your mind? Why not pull out that box of photos and look them over, treasuring each one and thanking your loving Father for his kindness to you?

2. Read the following verses and describe the differences between your goals as a parent and God's: Colossians 1:18–20; Ephesians 1:22–23; 4:15–16.

3. The end of the passage about Christ's self-emptying love is Philippians 2:9–11: "For this reason also, God highly exalted Him, and bestowed on Him the name which is above every name, so that at the name of Jesus every knee will bow, of those who are in heaven and on earth and under the earth, and that every tongue will confess that Jesus Christ is Lord, to the glory of God the Father." As mothers, it's easy for us to want our children to have a name that's highly esteemed, but that's not our place. What do these verses teach us about God's ultimate place of honor for his Son? What do they teach you about self-emptying love?

4. What divestitures are on your immediate horizon? What is most troubling to you about this process? What are you afraid to lose? Is it that change is difficult, or is there something even more disheartening in this season for you?

5. Read 2 Kings 21:19–22:2 and 2 Chronicles 28–29:2. What do these verses teach you about God's sovereign rule in the lives of your children? If your children are serving the Lord, is it because you were such a good witness?

6. Below you'll find one possible outline for a letter you might want to write to your children. Remember, you can adjust this format as you like to make it your own.

> Dear _____,
>
> As I've been thinking about how blessed I am to be your mother, it occurs to me that I may not have said that to you recently. _____, please know that I love you and that you will always be my child, no matter how far away we are from each other. Just as you were part of me once, growing beneath my heart, so you will be always in my heart, and for this I'm thankful.
>
> It's also occurred to me that, although I did love you, I sinned against you and, because of God's grace to me, I need to confess these sins to you. Please think about what I'm confessing, and don't just say, "Oh, Mom, it's okay!"

In what follows below, you can outline your areas of failure using the list on pages 74–75, adding or deleting as you see fit. Remember, avoid *if, but,* and *maybe.* Specifically confess any that are pertinent to you. If you can think of specific examples, that's the best. That way, your child will know that you're serious, not just trying to placate your conscience. Accept and recognize that there may be consequences to your sin, and allow your child time to think about what you've written and how he or she wants to respond. Finally, ask for forgiveness. You might say something like this, "In light of these, my sins, I'm asking you to forgive me. I know that might be hard for you right now, and I'm willing to wait to hear from you until you're ready. Please know that, in any case, I love you, am praying for you, and am seeking God's grace to change."

Feel free then to add anything that you might like as a way of closing salutation. Before you send this letter, please remember to spend time in prayer, confessing your sin to your Father and asking that his grace prepare your child's heart. Don't use this occasion to bring up any old offenses that your child committed and then trust the Lord to use this in his way for his glory, and don't demand that your child respond in the way you're hoping. Remember that this is something your Father has asked you to do, not a new method of manipulating your children to get them to do what you want them to do.

7. Summarize this chapter in three or four sentences.

five

Leaving Your Father and Mother

For this reason a man shall leave his father and his mother, and be joined to his wife. (Gen. 2:24)

From the time our children were young, splashing in the bathtub or shrieking as they ran through the sprinklers on a warm, summer's day, I've prayed about their marriages. I've prayed that the Lord would provide the right spouse for them: someone who would encourage them in godliness and relieve their burdens. "Lord," I've supplicated, "please bring them devout believers who will love them, who will cheer and care for them."

In the summer of 1995, our daughter, Jessica, became Mrs. Cody Thompson. Then, in the spring of 2000, her younger brother, Joel was blessed to receive Ruth Scipione as his bride. Phil and I have been gifted with these wonderful new additions to our family. We love, respect, and are grateful for

Cody and Ruth. They're learning to live with their spouses, and we're learning something new at the same time too: how to become godly in-laws. Phil and I are keenly aware that we're still growing in these new roles, and we hope that we're not making it too hard for them in the meantime.

The Counselor Counsels Herself

From time to time I've had opportunity to do premarital counseling.[1] I've sat down with starry-eyed young couples and tried to outfit them for the road ahead. One session is usually spent talking with them about what it means to "leave father and mother." I ordinarily instruct them to write a letter to their respective parents, thanking them for their care and outlining the ways that their relationship will change after their marriage. A wonderful example of that type of letter is found in Wayne Mack's *Preparing for Marriage God's Way,* parts of which I've excerpted below:

> Dear Mom and Dad,
>
> I want to thank you for your love and devotion to me as I was growing up. . . . At this time, a very important time in each of our lives, our relationship will change—not deteriorate but change, not disappear but be altered. . . . As a Christian I will always honor you, appreciate you, respect you, pray for you, commend you and seek to help you, but still God says I must leave. . . . From the time of our wedding onward _____ and I will become one flesh. . . . I ask you to help us to learn how to merge our two independent lives into a one-flesh relationship practically. . . . You have been given wisdom from God and from time to time,

we will be turning to you for counsel. When we do, we will take your counsel seriously, but under God we will think, search the Scriptures and pray, and determine God's will for ourselves. . . . We want you to be free to agree or disagree with us . . . and we want the same freedom. This will be hard for you.[2]

"This will be hard for you." Oh, how easy it was for me to give that counsel to others, and how difficult it is to give it to myself. The change from being the number one authority in my children's lives to stepping aside and encouraging them to form a separate family unit was daunting. Even now, as we've garnered some experience, it's still difficult to keep my opinions to myself. After all, doesn't mother know best?

In this chapter, we'll take a look at some of the changes that occur when your children marry, suggest some steps to help your children establish their families, view some pitfalls to avoid, and then offer a letter for you to write to your married children.

The First Wedding

God performed the first wedding, as he brought Eve to her husband, Adam. While Adam was filled with joy and delight at this reflection of himself, God immediately stepped in to communicate his regulations for all subsequent marriages. "Therefore a man shall leave his father and his mother and hold fast to his wife, and they shall become one flesh" (Gen. 2:24 ESV).

It is interesting, isn't it, that the first command God gives after he establishes marriage is one of leaving the former family? This fact points out the truth that a new family can't be properly developed until the old family is out of the picture. As Jay Adams writes, "Old ties cannot be broken unless there is 'leaving.' New ties cannot be established unless the old ones are gone."[3] In light of this truth, we need to be intentional about helping our children leave. After all, if we've prayed for them and taught them, now we need to let them learn to follow the Lord's commands, to lean on his strength and learn about his grace on their own. But this isn't easy, is it? Facing the realities of family life after our children leave to start their own lives is hard. It's so trying to step out of a role that's become so familiar and step into a new one . . . especially when we know that our way is best! When do I give my opinion? How much help should I offer? When is it right for me to tell them that they're making a mistake? How do I say no to them when they're in trouble . . . again? And how many times have I thwarted my prayers for them to grow in their marriages by offering too much advice or making things too easy for them?

All of these questions and thousands more like them tend to plague our thoughts. In the case of children with whom you have a good relationship, I know that it is particularly hard to stay out of their lives. My children are used to asking for and receiving my counsel, they love and respect me, and it's difficult for me to slip out of my role of the Bible Answer Mom into the lesser role of advisor. How am I supposed to keep my opinions to myself? I know them; I know what's best. Why can't I continue to guide them as I have all these years? Frequently these are the reasonings of my mind. It's hard to stand by and watch my children make choices that I think are unwise, and I'll bet that it's the same for you.

What Do You Mean, You Don't Need Me Anymore?

It's obvious that one reason why this transition is so difficult for me is that my heart is filled with pride, unbelief, and the desire to be needed by my children. On the off chance that it's the same for you, let's explore this struggle for a moment.

It is inherently arrogant for me to think that without me and my wisdom, my children will be doomed to failure and grief. This line of thinking reveals the self-sufficiency and pride that saturate my heart. Although I have been used by the Lord to nurture and discipline them, God has always been quite able to care for them without me, and he isn't worried about how he'll work in their lives now that I don't play such a prominent role. It's at times like this that I have to remember that they aren't my children anyway; I was just an interim manager.

The vexation that I feel at the prospect of these changes is also a sign of my unbelief. Do I trust the Lord with my children? Do I believe that God can providentially rule and overrule in their lives, guiding them by his great grace, protecting them from foolishness? Do I trust that even though he may allow them to make mistakes, he'll also wring immense good out of the situations that I worried and fretted over, growing them and teaching them to rely on him?

Another troublesome facet of letting them go is the fear that if I do, they won't need me any longer. Here's a reality that we all need to face: Motherhood is inherently fleeting. It is planned obsolescence. That's a scary thought for me, primarily because so much of my existence has been centered around and tied to my role as mother. Who am I if not James, Jessica, and Joel's mom? I've spent an afternoon or two wandering through our house, wondering what I'm supposed to be doing now. I've picked up the phone to call one of them, just to chat, and then realized that they're busy with their lives and they don't need to hear from me every day. My motivation in calling them is that I miss them and want to hear their voices. It's a habit of my heart. *Should I spend this time in a better way?* I wonder. Is there something else that the Lord has for me at this moment aside from pining for their voices?

I'm not saying that there isn't going to be any time when I'll be able to nurture or instruct them ever again. I'm just trying to point out the reality of life as the Lord has defined it. Every living thing grows and changes and leaves one family or group to start another. Why would we be any different?

I also need to understand what these changes teach me about God's love of multiplication and growth. As I've already said before, nothing in all of creation stays static. One of the first commands that God gave to Adam and Eve as he directed and defined their lives was to "be fruitful and multiply and fill the earth with fruit." How is that going to happen unless families split apart? Every cell in my body will split apart to create new living cells today. Think about this thought for a moment: Without this continual leaving and cleaving, all life would cease. Why do we think that our lives should be any different?

Father, we mothers should pray together, *please help our unbelief and humble us. Please cause us to believe that your plan for our children is better than anything we could ever think of. Please help us to see what you have planned for us to do now, who you would like us to nurture and love. Please help us to learn what it means to be silent and especially help us to see the good that you see in our children and their spouses. And help us to bow down before your throne again and pray with our suffering Lord, "Not my will, no, Lord, not even here."*

What Leaving Means to the One Left Behind

In light of the fact that my children are commanded to leave their parents and I'm commanded to love them, what steps should I take as I face their absence?

I will think and pray before offering them any advice.

I will not tell them what to do unless my husband and I are sure that they are about to violate the plain teaching of Scripture. There will be expected differences in style in their home. Perhaps they will share the workload differently or choose to attend a different church. These are their decisions, and as an autonomous family, seeking to fulfill God's specific calling on their lives, differences in choice or style are unimportant.

In every other case, we will not advise them unless they ask for our opinion. Even when they ask us for our opinion, there will be times when we will find ourselves in disagreement with their choice. It will be then that we will have to believe that perhaps their choice is the better one for them, and that even if it isn't, the Lord will use it in their lives for his glory and their good.

We will seek to avoid trying to save them or bail them out of every problem that they come upon. That doesn't mean that we can't, when we are able and when the need is there, help them. Our goal, however, must be to help them learn to lean on the Lord while encouraging them that we are standing behind them, praying for them all the way.

Our oldest grandchild, Wesley, is about to enter kindergarten. Because there are so many choices of schooling available to our daughter and her husband, she's asked me for my opinion in the matter, which I've given to her. I have also made it clear that although I would love to help them with Wesley's tuition, if they decide to send him to a Christian school, we won't be able to do so. We would love to be able to pay for all of our grandchildren's education, but we can't, and it wouldn't be right for us to pay for one and not offer to pay for others. This is a situation in which I would love to step in and take over. *I spent many years sacrificing for my children's education. I know what this is like. I know how to do this,* I think. But it wouldn't be appropriate for me to do this now. It would rob my children of the opportunity to learn the wonderful lessons the Lord has taught me.

Filling Up the Sufferings of Christ

I also recognize that there are undoubtedly women reading this book who don't have a close relationship with their children. Perhaps the relationship is pretty solid but they live at a great distance, or perhaps your relationship with them was never very strong, for whatever reason. Let's think about the special difficulties this time of life foists upon you.

At a conference I recently attended, a woman approached me after my teaching session. "My daughter and her husband are leaving for Ecuador in five months to do missions work. I'm trying to be glad that they're serving the Lord and that he'll be using them, but I'm also filled with sorrow and grief that I won't be able to see her every day anymore. I don't say anything about this to her because I want her to follow the Lord's leading, but my heart is breaking. Once they go, they won't be home for four years—it's just so far away. I don't know how I'll make it," she said as silent tears slid down her face. What could I say to her? How could I comfort her?

The apostle Paul had a view of his suffering that is quite foreign to many modern Christians. He said, "Now I rejoice in my sufferings for your sake, and in my flesh I do my share on behalf of His body, which is the church, in filling up what is lacking in Christ's afflictions" (Col. 1:24). What did Paul mean when he said that there was something lacking in Christ's afflictions that he was "filling up"?

We know what he didn't mean. He didn't mean that there was something lacking in Christ's atoning death on the cross. The Lord was right when he uttered those three most precious words, "It is finished." His substitutionary death in our place was complete at that moment, and he doesn't need anything from Paul the apostle or any of us to make it any more efficacious. All that needed to be done was done. *It is finished.*

But what does Paul mean when he says that his sufferings fill up what is lacking in Christ's afflictions? Primarily this: Although the atonement is complete and there is no longer any need to suffer for our sins, Christians are called upon to suffer for the sake of the gospel, so that others may come to know the truth. Every tear that you cry and every heartache you endure for the sake of those people in that foreign land is a filling up of the sufferings of Christ. As John Piper writes,

> Paul's sufferings complete Christ's afflictions *not* by adding anything to their worth, but by extending them to the people they were meant to save. What is lacking in the afflictions of Christ is not that they are deficient in worth, as though they could not sufficiently cover the sins of all who believe. What is lacking is that

91

the infinite value of Christ's afflictions is not known and trusted in the world. These afflictions and what they mean are still hidden to most peoples. And God's intention is that the mystery be revealed to all the nations. So the afflictions of Christ are "lacking" in the sense that they are not seen and known and loved among the nations. They must be carried by ministers of the word. And those ministers of the word "complete" what is lacking in the afflictions of Christ by extending them to others.[4]

Many times our releasing of our children to move across the country or around the world with their spouses is part and parcel of our "filling up the sufferings of Christ." Perhaps they aren't called to full-time ministry, as this woman's daughter had been; perhaps they're only relocating to secure the education or job they think that God is calling them to. Even in these seemingly commonplace decisions, your love, support, and release of them to follow Christ's call is part of your work for him. Do you see it that way? Do you love his kingdom and work this much?

Perhaps your married children haven't pulled up roots and transplanted themselves thousands of miles away . . . perhaps they live around the corner. Even in this circumstance, will you release them to find and fulfill God's claim on their lives—even if that's something different from what you've envisioned for them? Will you even encourage them to leave, if they believe it's God's will? These are hard questions, I know. They are questions that get to the heart of what I believe about God's plan for me—as a mother, as a valiant woman, as a daughter of the King. It also gets to the heart of what I believe about his character and the importance of his kingdom.

I know that your desire is to fulfill God's will for your life. Like all Christians, we long to hear the words, "Well done, good and faithful servant." Divestiture is painful, however, particularly when our children have made a home with someone else . . . someone whose opinions, tastes, and desires matter more than ours. This is painful and tearing for most mothers, even when we approve of and enjoy the spouses they've chosen. There have been times when I've found myself in a cellar of affliction because of the choices that my children or their mates have made. It's at that time that I have to remind myself, as the Puritan Samuel Rutherford said, that "when he was cast into the cellars of affliction, he remembered that the great King always kept his wine there."[5] What wonderful wine have you imbibed in this cellar of affliction? What joy and relief has it brought to your heart? What have you learned about Jesus and his perfections through this affliction?

Stepping to the Side of the Picture

Have you ever said to your children, "Your marriage is the most important relationship in your life"? Again, I trust that you believe that truth, but have you ever communicated it to your married children? How have you done that?

I wonder how many marriages have been tainted by the carping of a mother-in-law who wouldn't accept the fact that her daughter or son had left their father and mother. We mothers must make it a matter of highest priority never to allow or encourage disparaging speech or gossip about our children's spouses. Even worse, we must never criticize them or seek to undermine their place. That doesn't mean that we never speak into their lives. But if we have something to say that is important and godly, we should say it to both of them, and we should do so respecting the fact that they are a separate adult unit, no longer under our authority. May the Lord grant us the grace to do so and to repent of the times when we've neglected this parental responsibility.

It may be that you feel so much love for your child that you can't bear to let him or her leave. First Corinthians 13 is instructive in this situation, teaching us that authentic love is not self-focused but rather longs for the best for the beloved. The best for your son or daughter is a holy, loving, committed, one-flesh relationship with his or her spouse, where your child looks for guidance, encouragement, and comfort first from the Lord and second from the spouse. You're probably going to still be in the picture but not in the center of the frame—and this is the right and godly way for it to be.

Another Wedding to Plan For

At the end of this chapter I've written out a sample letter for you to consider using with your married children. In the meantime though, let me encourage you to think about the wonderful wedding that we'll all be a part of when our great King will bring us to his home for the feast that is to come. At this wonderful celebration, we'll be joined to our Savior, and we'll cleave to him and become one in spirit in a way that will make all of our afflictions here worthwhile. Live in the light of this truth as you ponder your relationship with your children and their spouses, rejoice in the Lord's wonderful plan for you, and joyfully release them to their new, God-designed reality.

1. Write out your present job description. Is there anything on that list that doesn't belong there now that you are the parent of a married couple?

2. What does "leave your father and mother" mean to you? What would it look like in your life?

3. Study 1 Peter 4:12–13, "Beloved, do not be surprised at the fiery ordeal among you, which comes upon you for your testing, as though some strange thing were happening to you; but to the degree that you share the sufferings of Christ, keep on rejoicing, so that also at the revelation of His glory you may rejoice with exultation." What would rejoicing in the participation in the sufferings of Christ look like in your life? How could you encourage your children in their desire to serve and lay down their lives for the Lord?

4. Prayerfully consider (with your husband, if you're married) writing a letter like the one below to your children. Please feel free to modify it in any way, making it your own.

> Dear _____,
>
> You know, it was ____ years ago that I first held you in my arms and lovingly looked into your little face. Your tiny hand was so small, and as I held you I knew that you needed me. I was so afraid that I wouldn't know what to do or how to be what you needed me to be. *How can I do this, Lord?* I wondered. There in your dependency, you needed me to feed you, to dress you, and to teach you how to walk and how to communicate. Later on, you needed me to instruct you in how to live your life. This was a role that I loved and cherished. But this is a role that I'm no longer

called to fulfill. Now that you and ____ are married, I need to learn a new role.

And in a very similar way to that day ____ years ago, I'm praying for strength and wisdom. *How do I do this, Lord?* I still wonder.

In Genesis 2:24, the Lord God instructed the first married couple to leave their father and mother. That's a command that's still in force today, and as I've thought about it and its ramifications for us, I can see that I haven't been doing what I'm supposed to do. There have been many times when I've [fill this part out with your own words. For instance, you could say, "I've given you money instead of teaching you to rely on the Lord's provision." "I've spoken in an unkind manner about your spouse to you (or with you); that's something that grieves God." "I've sought to advise you on matters that were not my concern, and tried to get you to build your new life according to my plan."]

These failures on my part to let you go and let you get on with building your own family were wrong. I'm asking you and ____ to forgive me for failing to see how God has changed our relationship and desiring to hold on to it for my own purposes.

Please don't think that I won't be there for you or that I won't still love you and cherish the times that we'll share together. It's just that now I'll be treating you as a fellow adult and giving you advice only when Dad and I think that you're sinning in some way or when you ask us for it. I want to encourage you to disagree with us, if you and ____ think that we're wrong. This won't affect our relationship or the fact that I love you. You no longer need to worry about my opinion or trying to please me.

It's been many years since I first received the gift that is you. I've been thankful for each of them, and I'm eagerly anticipating the delightful changes that will occur in the future. Please know that I'll always be your mom and that you can always count on me to pray for you and be there if you need me.

5. Summarize what you've learned from this chapter in four or five sentences.

six

Just Call Me "Mimi"!

*Then Naomi took the child and laid him in her
lap, and became his nurse. (Ruth 4:16)*

hink about the life of one afternoon woman,
Naomi. You'll recall how she had migrated
to Moab with her husband and two sons to
escape a famine. I can imagine that although she missed her
family and friends from Bethlehem, she was comforted by the
presence of her husband and sons and thoughts of her new life
with them. But soon her existence took on a more somber garb.
Her husband died. Still, though, even in her grief, she had the
consolation of her sons, and as they married, she hoped that
she would soon have grandchildren to cheer her heart. But this
was not the Lord's plan for her. Within ten years, Naomi found
herself bereft of even her dear sons, and she prepared to return
to Bethlehem an empty, broken woman.

Could this be Naomi? her friends wondered as she approached her town with Ruth, her daughter-in-law. " 'Don't call me Naomi,' she told them. 'Call me Mara, because the Almighty has made my life very bitter. I went away full, but the LORD has brought me back empty. Why call me Naomi? The LORD has afflicted me; the Almighty has brought misfortune upon me' " (Ruth 1:20–21 NIV).

Unlike today, in ancient times one's name represented one's nature. For instance, Naomi meant "agreeableness, delight, splendor, or grace."[1] Her previous life had been delightful and agreeable: she had a husband and two sons, and although they were experiencing famine, she still knew their comfort and protection. But when she returned from Moab, in emptiness and bitterness she instructed her former acquaintances to call her Mara, a name that means "bitterness." Naomi had been stripped and felt empty and ashamed, but her story wasn't over. Returning with her from the land of bereavement was her daughter-in-law, Ruth, through whom the Lord would providentially bring her joy again.

Think about the verse at the beginning of this chapter: "Then Naomi took the child and laid him in her lap, and became his nurse" (Ruth 4:16). I think that it would be easy for us to overlook the import of these words. This is a woman who had become convinced that the forecast for her life was only bitter hardness; that was until the Lord turned her captivity and gave her a grandson—Obed. The verses before the one referenced above read, "Then the women said to Naomi, "Blessed is the LORD who has not left you without a redeemer today, and may his name become famous in Israel. May he also be to you a restorer of life and a sustainer of your old age; for your daughter-in-law, who loves you and is better to you than seven sons, has given birth to him" (Ruth 4:14–15).

Naomi's friends were rejoicing for her because of Boaz and Ruth's kindness. She would again know the care and sustaining of a loving son. But their joy for her didn't stop with Ruth and Boaz. They were also rejoicing in the birth of her grandson. Obed too was a gift from the Lord to her and would renew her life and sustain her in her old age. And in one way, that's what grandchildren do—they renew our life and will fulfill us in our old age.

Been There, Done That

I can remember a friend telling me about the great joy of being a grandparent. "Yeah, yeah," I thought, "I've been there, done that. I know what having kids is all about." And then . . . Wesley was born, and my life became pleasant and delightful again. At the time of this writing, I have two delightful little grandsons, Wesley, who is four, and Hayden, who is two; and two granddaughters, Eowyn, who isn't yet one, and Alexandria, who will be born in just two months (Lord willing). Want to see a picture? Ah, life is beautiful.

I've tried to understand why grandparenting is so special, so blessed. I know all the typical reasons, and some of them are right. It's true that I can spoil them and then send them home. It's true that I have resources now, both time and money, to spend on them that I didn't have before, when my kids were young. In some ways the pressure to perform is off, and I'm freer to just enjoy them. But, at least for me, there is something else. There's a rediscovery of a joy that's been gone for many years. There's the renewed opportunity to nurture new life— something that I had to give up several years ago. I'm not saying that I've been Mara or dissatisfied. What I am saying is that the joy that was ours when we held our little ones in our arms and then dissipated as they grew older is back now, and in spades. Do you doubt what I say? Ask any afternoon woman you know about her grandchildren and watch her light up.

Grandchildren are the reintroduction of new life and joy—a time to do everything that you couldn't do before, but this time without the fear and pressure that sometimes accompanies parenthood. When Wesley, a.k.a. "my darling," called me "Mimi," I became a new person. Who am I? I'm not Elyse Fitzpatrick, writer or conference speaker. I'm Meem (the boys' nickname for me). These little treasures could call me anything that they wanted and I would still come running. They've got my heart, and I couldn't be more blessed.

I've had to learn all the new rules for pregnancy and childcare. Pregnant women no longer drink caffeine or take any form of over-the-counter medicine. I shudder to think what was pumping through my bloodstream and into my babies' bodies when I was pregnant. I've had to learn how to properly install a car seat; no more throwing them in the back seat and hoping for the best. I've also learned about gaze aversion and restricting the intake of honey (I keep thinking "Oops!"). They have sunglasses for babies so they aren't exposed to too many UV rays. I've learned not to give them real Cheerios because they're so firm they might cause choking, and I've taken a CPR class and have the Steps to Take in Case of Choking poster in my laundry room. I recently considered buying a very large SUV that had three rows of seats and a DVD player with headphones in the back. We could call it the Mimi Mobile!

I know that some women look at the afternoon of life as a time to buy a spiffy new sports car and a small condo so that they can live in style and privacy through their remaining years. But it's not that way for me—at least not yet. The joys I've known at being a grandmother have been more than I can tell.

Sorrow and Heartache

According to a survey done by AARP, about 78 percent of "grand-boomers" get to see their grandchildren between once a week and once a month.[2] But I know that for many women, there's sorrow here too. I'm aware that there are many women who rarely see their grandchildren. Perhaps they live across the country, or their relationship with their children is strained and they don't get to have input into their lives. I can only imagine the heartache that would accompany the birth of a new grandchild that you know you'll rarely get to hold. I also know that there are numbers of women whose grown children live the kind of lifestyle that brings them heartache and shame, while they worry about the health and safety of their precious little ones.

Below you'll find stories written by two afternoon friends of mine. Kathie, a dear sister whose difficulties with her daughter and grandchildren touched my heart, writes the first one. The second one, written by Juliette, spoke deeply to me about sacrifice and a grandmother's willingness to be a parent to her grandchildren. Let the stories of these women encourage you and grant you a new perspective of God's power.

Our first grandchild, Andrew, was born to our second *Kathie's Story* daughter fourteen years ago. Anne, Andrew's mother, was eighteen and unmarried. I don't think any parent is ever ready to hear from their unmarried daughter that she is pregnant. But our God is so good. The very moment Anne told me about her pregnancy, the Lord was there giving me a sense of calm and assurance.

Anne and Andrew lived with us until Andrew was five months old. At that time Anne wanted to move in with a new boyfriend and put Andrew up for adoption. My husband, Ted, and I knew that God had placed Andrew in our family. We told Anne that we couldn't keep her from moving out, but we would not allow Andrew to be put up for adoption.

During the next several years Anne was in and out of Andrew's life. I would take our relationship with Anne and Andrew's situation to the Lord in prayer, but then I was so sure that I knew what was best I would set about trying to fix and control everything. I frequently laid my burdens at the foot of the cross, just to snatch them back.

When Andrew was four, Anne married, and she and her husband had a little girl. A few years later, Anne asked if we would let Andrew come live with them. All through this I was absolutely sure that no one could possibly love Andrew as much as I did. Certainly no one could protect him like I could! But when Andrew was eight, the Lord convicted me that I needed to let him go. I was heartbroken when he left, but John 3:16 kept coming back to me. Having Andrew move away was nothing compared with God giving up his only Son to die on a cross. And I had God's assurance, through his Word, that he would never leave or forsake me.

Since that time, Ted and I have been blessed with six beautiful grandchildren. Anne now has four children. Her boyfriend is the father of her last two little girls. He is verbally and physically abusive and in and out of their life. We are fairly certain that Anne and the boyfriend abuse drugs.

God's Goodness in My Difficulty

Sitting and looking back on coming to peace with my grandchildren being reared by parents who are not walking with the Lord, I am flooded with memories of God working on my heart. He used his Word, the counsel of Christian friends, books on his character, Bible study groups, and the preaching of his Word.

During a time in which Anne wouldn't let us see or even talk on the phone with Andrew or her daughter, Ellie, I was devastated. I wanted to rescue and to lash back. I wanted control of the situation and revenge. A Christian friend told me that God loved my grandchildren more than I do. In light of this truth, I went back to Matthew 10:29–31, where Jesus teaches that even a sparrow's fall is controlled by God's will and that our heavenly Father knows even the number of hairs on our head. At about the same time I was reading *When God Weeps* by Joni Eareckson Tada and Steven Estes.[3] In this book the authors tell of children being reared under horrible circumstances. While God weeps about the depravity that leads to those circumstances, he also can use them to build a loving relationship with him. These truths were encouraging to me during this dark time in my life.

During this time, Barbara, another friend, and I were sharing some of the actions of our grown children and how they were affecting our grandchildren. Barb made the comment, "We just have to love 'em." At first I thought she was using a cliché and being flip, but after praying about it, I realized she was sharing God's truth with me. After praying for God to give me the grace to love my daughter, he not only softened my heart but also gave me opportunities to demonstrate that love to her.

Later on, during a Bible study group, I understood Jeremiah 17:9, "The heart is deceitful above all things and desperately wicked; who can know it?" (NKJV) in the light of my context. While my heart may tell me what is best for my grandchildren, I can't trust that feeling. Only God knows what is best for them, and I can trust him. I've since learned that when I am willing to give up my desire for control of my grandchildren's situations, he is faithful to bless me with a sense of peace and contentment.

I've also come to realize that while I was worried about saving my grandchildren in an earthly sense, it is their eternal salvation that is truly important. Only Christ can do that. This has convicted me to be more diligent in my prayers for my children, not just Anne, but for all my children and grandchildren.

The Lord also used my pastor to speak truth into my heart. While he was preaching on the Book of Romans, I rediscovered Romans 8:28. This was God's promise to me personally! He is working all things for my good and more importantly, his glory. My prayer is that he will be glorified in my life, in the lives of my children, and the lives of my grandchildren.

Mothering Your Grandchildren

A few years ago I met a woman who was my age but who had custody of her daughter's two- and four-year-old children. As I listened to her story and the joy with which she was approaching this repeat of mothering, I was encouraged—but

I also wondered about the breadth of this problem. According to the 2000 census, there are five and a half million grandparents living in households with grandchildren. Of this number, a little less than half (2,352,724) are responsible for raising and providing for them.[4] In 1997, there were almost four million children being cared for by their grandparents, a number that is up 76 percent from 1970.

No one who is aware of the cultural trends in America should be surprised about these figures. Although some children live with their grandparents due to their parents' deaths, the majority of children who come under our care are there because of substance abuse, teen pregnancies, incarceration of parents, or family violence. If you or someone you know is in this situation, perhaps the story that follows will be an encouragement to you.

Children or Grandchildren? *Juliette's Story*

The Lord delivered our two kidlets to us four years ago. When the children were twenty-five and nineteen months old, God had rescued them from the eerie dark world of drugs, alcohol, and mutual combat between their mom and dad. The day they arrived at our home forever changed the way we would live from that point on. There was no warning, no conversations between the mom and dad and us. And, although looking back I can see that God had been preparing us for this momentous event long before it happened, never, never would I have imagined this would be my role at age fifty-five after rearing five children of our own who were all well into their thirties. Well, it did happen, and we've been receiving the blessings ever since. From the first moment, the Lord poured out his grace and mercy on this family and quickly made it clear we were in for the long haul.

My husband and I have learned many lessons along the way—only through God's grace—that have been a source of encouragement to us day by day. It was immediately apparent that Jeremy and Jeannie had no structure on which to rely. So, the first thing we did was to start scheduling activities at the same time every day—every hour in some cases—day after day—devoting ourselves entirely to them. Touching, talking, bathing, feeding, napping, and especially outdoor activities (which are very important to kids who rarely saw the light of day), shopping, reading, holding—all these became habitual and comforting to the kids as they settled in. To this day, they rely on that assurance from us—and contentment seems to ooze from and overflow their little hearts.

Dealing with their mom and dad was very difficult at first. They, of course, assumed they could "clean up" and then get the kids back and everything would be fine. Not so. We felt it was vital that we secure legal guardianship, once we learned that their mother was making plans to leave the city and take the kids with her. Securing that legal guardianship was an important step in securing the safety and future of the kids. We had immediately taken the view that in order to do a proper job with the kids— no matter how long they would be with us—we mustn't think it was temporary, but rather a permanent arrangement. Pursuing guardianship can be costly, as it was for us, in terms of finance and relationships with the birth mom and dad. But in the long term, it gave us parental rights, and we could then be free to rear the kids as we felt best.

So, who are we to the kids . . . are we their parents or grandparents? We believed it was best to be truly honest with the kids with everything. We've taught them what a parent is and that a parent isn't necessarily a mom or dad. They know us as their parents, call us Grams and Grandpa, and know they have a birth mom and dad. Now they know their role in the family, and that is what brings them contentment. We've kept a dialogue going with the mother and father (and, in fact, the other set of grandparents) so that, once again, the kids will see how they fit into the whole family. That dialogue is important (they see the kids about twice a year), so that as the children move into their adolescent years and more questions come up about why their mom and dad aren't living with them, they will have a frame of reference. God is so wise. He uses the lives of their parents as a witness of his wonderful covenantal promise—blessings for obedience and curses for disobedience. Our grandchildren are learning these important lessons even today.

What has suffered somewhat over these past years is our relationship with our other five grandchildren, some of whom are older than our little kidlets. In light of this strain, we've tried to have this whole tribe together often. We're balancing the truth that we must be parents to our kids but grandparents to the others. It is difficult at times to separate the two, and I know the others yearn for more time with us on their terms. We try to schedule time alone with them, but this is never nearly enough.

Fitness is another vital part of rearing grandchildren. I'm speaking of the grandparents and our kids. We strive to keep healthy, fit, and active so that they don't become fearful of us getting "too old" to care for them. And we include them in all our activities. They seem to thrive as we explore the outdoors and pursue our favorite sports.

Oh, the great joy of living with little ones again! At this age, we have the resources, God-given wisdom, and patience that were really in short supply rearing our own five kids. We're very careful to guard against thoughts of resentment that might creep into our minds. It would be unacceptable for us to think that these precious little ones would suffer from our sinful attitudes. God has given us this season to bring up his children under his nurture and admonition.

The Long Arm of the Grandmother

I remember a time when our youngest son, Joel, was thinking about getting an earring. Phil and I didn't approve, but we didn't think that it would have been sinful for him to do so, so we told him our concerns and then left it up to him. After a short time he came back to us and said, "I've decided not to get the earring." (We breathed a sigh of relief.) "After all," he said, "what would I say to grandma?" Our son was feeling his grandmother's influence, and that's not unusual; in fact, we have a biblical example of the long arm of the grandmother.

There was once a young man whose father was an unbeliever but whose mother and grandmother were believers. God used their faith as the means to bring salvation to this young man. The young man? Timothy, the protégé of the apostle Paul. Remember what Paul wrote to Timothy, "For I am mindful of the sincere faith within you, which first dwelt in your grandmother Lois and your mother Eunice, and I am sure that it is in you as well" (2 Tim. 1:5).

I can imagine that Timothy's grandmother, Lois, was a woman who was concerned about the welfare of her dear grandson. He was a shy and retiring young man who wanted to follow the laws of Jehovah, but his father wouldn't allow him to be circumcised. *What will happen to his faith?* Lois undoubtedly wondered. But God had a plan for Timothy and was able to save him even though his father wasn't a believer. You and I can take heart that God can use us to bring our grandchildren to himself, or he can use another minister of the gospel. You can rest assured, though, that the Lord has the situation in control and that he hears the supplications borne of love from a grandmother's heart.

It seems that children are naturally drawn to the boundless love that flows through their grandmother, doesn't it? I've often thought that there isn't anyone else in the world who jumps up and down and cheers when they see me coming, and in my heart, I'm doing the same thing when I see them! As a valiant afternoon woman, I desire to be the kind of grandmother who influences these precious little ones for the Lord I love. I would imagine that's your desire as well. With our dear grandchildren, we have a great opportunity and open door. These little ones sense the love and commitment that we have for them, and they're merely responding in kind. These are precious years, and whatever the circumstance you find yourself in, the Lord can use your influence to impact their souls for eternity.

1. What is your relationship with your grandchildren like?

2. How diligent have you been to share the gospel with them and influence them for Christ?

3. What do you see your responsibilities to be? What are the challenges of the relationship?

4. If you don't already do so, begin today to pray daily for their souls. Write out your concerns and prayer for each of them.

5. Summarize what you've learned in this chapter in three or four sentences.

seven

When the Children Return Home

Train up a child in the way he should go,
even when he is old he will not depart from it.
(Prov. 22:6)

As I sat in the airport, listening for the boarding announcement,  I was equally torn between joy and sadness. Our eldest daughter, Melissa, was about to leave for college, a sad day that every parent dreams about, plans for, and looks forward to from the first day that that adorable little child leaps right into their hearts. It's also a day that every parent dreads, the day when that little being is supposedly ready to step out into the world on her own.

The school that our daughter was going to attend was in the southeast, on the opposite side of the country from San Diego, where she had lived her entire life. As I sat there vacillating between joy and excitement that our firstborn was going off to college and the heart-wrenching sadness having her leave our cozy little family unit brought, I began to cry. As that inevitable river of tears began flowing down my face, another one of my daughters came over to comfort me. She put her arm around my shoulder, and with great compassion she leaned over and said, "Don't worry, Mom, I'll never leave you." Instantly I was jolted out of my puddle of self-pity, moved by the tenderness and compassion my daughter was showing me. I was comforted, yet the absurdity of her statement brought laughter to my heart! As I looked up at her we both smiled. I giggled and hugged her and responded, "Of course you will—that's what you're supposed to do. It's just that moms are always sad when their children leave."

Although that might not be true for every parent, especially if they've had a difficult relationship with their child, it is normal to feel some degree of sadness when the child reaches adulthood and leaves. Why is this?

Let me introduce myself. I'm Vickie, and all through my adult years I've thought of myself as Vickie, the mother of three lovely daughters. Now that all three of them have become adults, they have gone their own way. What does the Bible say about children leaving their childhood home?

As you've already read in earlier chapters, God clearly states that it is his plan that a child leave father and mother and cleave to their spouse (Gen. 2:24). In addition to this verse, what other Scriptures might we learn from?

One of my favorite verses on child rearing has been Proverbs 22:6, "Train up a child in the way he should go, even when he is old he will not depart from it." As our children were growing up, we often discussed this verse, focusing on the "training up" perspective. We discussed why they needed the discipline that we hoped would train them in the right way. But now that the three of them are grown, the verse speaks to me of a different truth. Now I've put the emphasis on the part of that verse that says, "in the way he should go." I've recognized that although I was obligated to "train them up in the way they should go," now this time for training has ended and the time for letting them go has come. Here's where we parents often stumble and the sadness comes in. Letting them go requires change, and because we're creatures of habit we often feel discomfort with change. We stumble with worry and fear when we forget to put our trust in God while this parent-child relationship evolves to the next level: a parent–adult child fellowship. Although this change is hard, isn't it what should naturally take place? We can also rejoice if God has helped us do our job and train our child in the right way, that he or she is now ready to go on his way, which will also be God's way. This makes our children not only our children but also our brothers and sisters in the Lord.

Comings and Goings in Our Little Home

This was the foundation that had been laid in our home when our daughter left for college. During Melissa's course of study, we talked on the phone regularly, and she returned home often for holiday visits. Over the time that Melissa was gone, our second daughter, Christa, remained at home and attended a local Bible college. The year that Melissa graduated with her bachelor's degree, our youngest daughter, Jessica, graduated from high school. Like her sister, she too chose to stay home and attend Bible college. Although Melissa had graduated from college, she wasn't sure what she wanted to do with her degree, so she decided to move back home. *Great!* I thought. *Our cozy little family unit was back intact.* But was it really?

The girls were all adults now, and as happy as we were that they had chosen to live with us, we all had to learn how to live together in a house made up of all adults. As usual, change was slow and difficult in our home. Not only did we have to learn to deal with adult daughters, but also our lives were further complicated by my mother living at home with us, as she suffered with Alzheimer's disease. By the time Melissa had moved back home, my mother was a complete invalid. I will always be grateful to the girls because they chose to stay at home and help care for their grandmother. Caring for my mom became the consuming focus of our family, and though it was stressful, everyone's schedules were flexible enough that someone could always be at home with her. With God's grace and my family's willingness to be his servants by caring for my mother, we were able to make it through that difficult time in faith. It was not until after my mother had passed away that my husband and I began to feel negative effects of our daughters' coming to adulthood and seeking to spread their wings.

It seemed to us that overnight our youngest daughter, Jessica, met the man she would one day marry, our eldest daughter, Melissa, became focused on her career, and our middle daughter, Christa, began questioning the direction of her life while she finished her final year in Bible college. It was as if they were all leaving the nest at once, or so my husband and I thought.

But I'm an Adult Now!

There we were, a happy family with three adult daughters, all living at home under one roof. Until then, our family life had run with relative smoothness, but now, with each of them focusing on her personal goals, things began to get difficult. The girls' lives were becoming more and more hectic. They were all working, two of them were still going to school, and their social lives were blossoming. They weren't spending as much time at home as they had in the past. This is where the road became rocky for us—or should I say especially for me? I, like other moms, was the household manager of our family. This meant that I knew the why, what, where, when, and how of everyone's schedule so that I could keep things flowing smoothly. The girls no longer saw this superintending as helpful. In fact, they found it to be intrusive and unnecessary.

Understanding the Way They Should Go

The first major change that my husband and I had to adjust to was understanding that the girls had lives of their own now. Remember our verse in Proverbs, "Train up a child in the way he should go, even when he is old he will not depart from it"? We discovered that our children were now struggling to go their own way. As parents, we had sought to be obedient to the Lord and his Word while we were raising our children. But now we had to be obedient to him in another way: We had to demonstrate faith in God and trust him enough to step out of the way so that our children could do what we had trained them to do. We had to let them go in the way they should go. For us, this was easier said than done. It was during this struggle that more of my favorite verses became even more special to me. Proverbs 3:5–6 reads, "Trust in the LORD with all your heart and do not lean on your own understanding. In all your ways acknowledge Him, and He will make your paths straight."

Our failure to step out of the way when our children reached the time when they were ready to go showed a lack of faith in God and might even have made our girls stumble or caused them to be tempted to sin. If we are truly trying to live our lives according to God's direction, then we have to come to the place where we pray, *Thank you, God, for the gift you've given us in our children. I now give them back to you, and I trust you that your will will be done in their lives.*

In praying in this way, we didn't mean that they were ever out of God's hand or that his will wasn't happening in their lives but that as parents we had forgotten this, and this lapse was making letting go even more troublesome.

In Genesis 22, we can see the faith it takes to obey God when it hurts. Abraham, the father of our faith, was put to the test in a much more difficult way. God told Abraham, "Take now your son, your only son, whom you love, Isaac, and go to the land of Moriah, and offer him there as a burnt offering on one of the mountains of which I will tell you" (Gen. 22:2).

God commanded Abraham to take Isaac, his son, the gift that God had so miraculously given him, and sacrifice him as a burnt offering! While we don't see the struggle that Abraham had with this, I can't imagine that he got much sleep that night. Scripture tells us that he was obedient even to the point of laying his dear son on the altar and raising a knife to slay him, before God stopped him and gave him a way of escape. That was true faith! And that is the kind of faith that we are to have as parents. Even if circumstances don't seem to be what we want for our children, we are called to trust God to provide the way of escape.

As our girls matured, they no longer found it helpful for me to know everything about their schedules. *We're adults now, and we don't want you to tell us what to do. You need to let us make our own decisions.* For my husband and me, this proved to be quite challenging. Where should the boundaries be? Did we have the right to place a curfew on them? Should we expect them to tell us of their plans? Was it proper for us to require them to do household chores? What about money? Should we still support them, or should they pay rent?

The Trials of Having Adult Children Living at Home

To find the answer to each of these questions, we persevered in prayer and worked through the situations that came about in our daily lives together. The first of these situations occurred when Jessica began a serious

119

relationship with the young man who is now her husband. This was new ground for us and was especially difficult for Cliff, my husband. The idea that one of our daughters was thinking of marriage came as quite a shock to him.

Jessica was only nineteen at the time, and her boyfriend, Zack, was only twenty. We had reservations because they were so young, and their relationship seemed to be in high gear, so Cliff stepped in. Since they were both in Bible college, studying to be in full-time ministry someday, and were both leaders in our church's youth group, Cliff set some clear boundaries and held them to high standards. He told them that their relationship needed to be above reproach, and that as leaders to the youth, they should serve as examples of what a godly relationship should be (1 Tim. 3:2). His advice to them was scripturally sound and came from the heart of a loving father who wanted the best for his beloved daughter and possible future son-in-law. But when you're so young and very much in love, rules to live by are not so easy to heed, even when you do love the Lord (Heb. 12:11). This was the case with Jessica. She resented our parental interference, felt that her father was being too hard, too controlling. She insisted that she was an adult and that she could make her own decisions. Needless to say, it was a trying time for all of us. It seemed that our family had been thrown into a constant state of turmoil.

The resentment that Jessica and Zack held seemed to be growing, while at the same time our two other daughters were going through life changes of their own. Both of them had new jobs, and everyone's schedule was different. We weren't able to have meals together, we were rarely home at the same time, and the idea that their little sister was about to get married and leave home was a difficult reality for them to grasp. During this time if I asked any of them to help out with household chores, the request was almost certainly met with an ungodly attitude or an argument. *What had happened to our happy little family?* I wondered. I was at my wits' end. I needed a reprieve, so in my prayer time I cried out to God. He provided a way of escape, and it came in the form of a phone call from Brazil.

For many years I have worked with foreign students, and our family has hosted students from around the globe. At the very time that I was praying, one of our students from Brazil called because she was missing us and asked me, "When is Jessica going to come and visit us?"

Melissa had gone to Japan for four months to visit friends when she had graduated from high school, and Christa had gone to Japan and Brazil. We had promised Jessica a trip to Brazil when she graduated from high school, but my mother's illness had prevented it. Jessica was the only member of our family who hadn't traveled abroad, something that we believe is important in helping us appreciate all that God has blessed us with. So my husband and I sat down with Jessica and offered her a trip to Brazil, explaining to her that if she was going to get married soon, we felt it was important for her to have this experience now, while she still could. She agreed, and Melissa offered to go with her as their last big fling as sisters before Jessica's marriage.

Although both the girls were excited, Zack wasn't. He was angry that we were sending Jessica away. His anger showed in his attitude toward us, so we made an appointment with our pastor. Cliff told our pastor that we had seen attitudes in Zack and Jessica that demonstrated that the relationship wasn't going in the right direction. Cliff didn't think he would be able to give his blessing to the relationship continuing, let alone culminating in marriage. Our pastor agreed to talk with Zack for us. In his kindness, God used this talk to change Zack's heart. It was a pivotal time in his life, and his attitude changed so completely while Jessica was gone that we could hardly believe it. God also used that time to change us. We realized that our daughters were now grown and while we would always be their parents, the way that we treated them needed to change. So we set up some guidelines that would help our home run more smoothly.

Our Guidelines

First we reminded the girls that although our relationship was changing, we were still their parents. This meant that God's command to them to "honor their father and mother" (Deut. 5:16; Eph. 6:2) still applied to them. This command from God is found in the Old and New Testaments, indicating how important it is to him. As parents, we thought that this verse merely inferred obedience, but it has a much deeper meaning than that. It is talking about the manner in which children treat their parents, showing them respect and honoring them by the way that they live. We told our daughters that they were welcome to live in our home as long as they wanted, and that while it is their home, it is our house. We expected them to be respectful of that fact and of us.

Second, we decided that now that they were adults, there would be no free ride. Since they all had jobs, they were to contribute to the household expenses. As parents, we felt that this would help them become more responsible, so we established an equitable amount they would pay each month for the room and board they were receiving.

Two of the most sensitive issues that we had to work out had to do with them letting us know their schedules and helping us out with the household chores. We dealt with the issues of coming and going by addressing it as a matter of common courtesy. Matthew 7:12 reads, "In everything, therefore, treat people the same way you want them to treat you, for this is the Law and the Prophets."

We were merely asking that the girls treat us the way that they wanted to be treated. Having the girls inform us of their schedule continued to be quite a sensitive issue until one specific occurrence. I had stopped after church on my way home to visit a friend. Because I was there much longer than I had intended to be and no one knew where I was, when I walked in the door both girls jumped to their feet demanding, "Where have you been?" While I never pointed out the obvious, I simply apologized for not calling home to let them know my plans. Now it seems as though communication isn't such a problem any more. I think that we all learned from that incident, because the girls have become more willing to let me know their plans and I've become less inquisitive and anxious over knowing theirs.

Helping with household chores is something we're all still working on. Everyone does their own laundry, and the kitchen chores are being worked out as we learn to serve each other.

Our Changing Roles

As parents of adult children, we have grown and learned that our roles are no longer what they once were. No longer do we need to "train them up in the way they should go"—that part of our relationship is over. Now our role is to be supportive and encouraging, just as our heavenly Father doesn't deal harshly with us but rather patiently waits for the fruit of the Spirit to be borne in our lives.

At this writing, Zack and Jessica have been married and living on their own for nearly four years, and they have recently become parents. While our other two daughters have chosen a different way they should go, they have decided to live here with us. Each has her reasons for staying home, and neither plans to live with us indefinitely. We have learned to let them live their lives and are comfortable with waiting for them to invite us in when they feel the need. We usually get along very well and enjoy each other's company. One of the girls gave me a card the other day that says it best. It read

Sometimes I need a mom,
Sometimes I need a friend,
Always I need you,
Have a happy day, mom.
We are a family and we need each other.

As the mother of three grown children and a temporary step-mom to a nephew, each of whom has moved in and out from time to time, I really enjoyed Vickie's story. I know that for many families, even though having adult children move back in may be a trying time, things frequently do work out in the end. But what about the woman who dreads the day that her son or daughter will ask for another opportunity to move back in with the family? How should we valiant afternoon women handle the phone call from the wayward child who has broken your heart before?

Hospitality without Regrets

Throughout this book, I've tried to emphasize that the home is primarily the residence of the husband and wife (not the wife and the children) and that particularly as children become adults, this understanding should increase. I'm reiterating this because mothers, it seems, are particularly prone to allowing their wayward children back in the home, hoping to repair relationship breaches that may have continued for years, without giving such a decision much forethought. A wise woman, therefore, will have long and reasoned discussions with her husband (or church leaders if she isn't married) before she says yes to allowing her little darling to move home. A more objective perspective will help you make sound decisions and may protect you from further grief. The counsel that you should receive before allowing the return of your prodigal should include setting ground rules, perhaps even in the form of written contracts, that include the following.

What is the purpose of this temporary arrangement? Is the child finishing school, changing careers, going through a divorce or the death of a spouse?

How long will this living arrangement last? Before allowing a child to move home, you should have some sort of end game in mind. For instance, if the child is finishing some specific schooling, how long will that take and when should the parent expect the child to be on his or her own again? Perhaps the child has had problems with drug or alcohol abuse, and you're willing to help her or him until she or he goes through a program of biblical counseling and gets a steady job again. In any case, whatever the circumstances, the child should not assume that you've opened your home indefinitely.

Will the child pay rent, or will she or he cover the added expense of having her or him live there? As I write this, my nephew, who has lived with my husband and me on several occasions, is living in the motor home in our driveway. We're letting him live there rent-free for a time because he's giving us all his money (except what he needs to live on) to save for him, as he is trying to put away enough to move to northern California. He understands that this arrangement is temporary and that if he doesn't deposit the bulk of his money in savings, the arrangement will change. I'm saying all of this because I think there are times when you might allow a child to live rent-free, but that shouldn't be the norm. Nor do I think that it helps a child to live off his parents, but rather does him a disservice. With a child who has been difficult in the past, settling exactly how much, what for, and when is essential.

What will your behavioral requirements be? As Vickie pointed out earlier in the chapter, her daughters were required to speak in a respectful manner and to let the family know their schedule. This would be the minimum requirement that I think wisdom would dictate. Whether you also want to establish a reasonable curfew would depend on the child's present problems and whether you're able to sleep at night when you don't know what time he or she will be home. Certainly rules about friends, noise, and chores should be set out.

What will your spiritual requirements be? Our nephew knows that if he is going to live with us, he's going to go to church with us. Since his employment was in a state of flux when he moved in, we told him that he should try to find a job that would not require him to work on Sundays. We recognized that sometimes this isn't possible, but we wanted him to know what our priorities are. I don't think that it's too much to ask that a child attend church with you at least on Sunday, and if a child isn't willing to acquiesce in this matter, the feasibility of the move is in great doubt anyway. Although that's hard, it's better to know up front than to go through great woe later.

What will the deal breakers be? Clearly establish from the beginning what behaviors would necessitate the child's immediately vacating your home. For example, illegal activity such as drug abuse or stealing should probably be one of the instances. Belligerent or abusive behavior or refusing to respect the authority God has placed in the home might also require an eviction, as should lying.

Each of these topics should be discussed before any living agreements are made and, if necessary, contracts may be signed. Your child should know what to expect from you—what you're willing to provide—and what's to be expected from him or her. Don't forget: In your desperation to reestablish a relationship with a wayward son or daughter, don't be duped into thinking that avoiding difficult but necessary subjects will make everything work out in the end.

One of the greatest joys in my afternoon years is the relationship I have with my adult children. There have been several times when we've opened our doors to allow them to return, and like Vickie, we've had pretty good success. I will say that the times of greatest difficulty between us was when we failed to communicate our expectations from the start. I know that I've foolishly avoided such conversations in the past because I'm hoping for some part of our relationship to change. I need to try to remember that the Lord may use the structure in our home to comfort and woo my children, and it is wise for you to do so also. Remember, he loves them more than you do.

1. Write out Proverbs 22:6. What new meaning about this well-known verse has Vickie's writing brought you?

2. What has your experience with children been like? In what ways can you relate to Vickie's? What have you done differently?

3. Meditate on Proverbs 3:5–6: "Trust in the LORD with all your heart and do not lean on your own understanding. In all your ways acknowledge Him, and He will make your paths straight." How would trusting in the Lord with all your heart change the way that you're presently handling having your children at home? How can you acknowledge God in all your ways? What is the promise that is here for you as you learn to trust, lean on, and acknowledge God?

4. How does the story of Abraham in Genesis 22 encourage you? Do you see the connection between Abraham's sacrifice and the great sacrifice of God's own dear Son? How does this encourage you as a woman whose role as mother has changed?

5. Summarize what you've learned in this chapter in three or four sentences.

eight

Dear Unbelieving Child, How I Long for Your Soul

I have no greater joy than this, to hear of my children walking in the truth. (3 John 1:4)

n this chapter, Eileen Scipione (my son, Joel's, mother-in-law) writes of her experiences with unbelieving children. Eileen and her husband, George, are godly parents who have experienced deep suffering at the current lack of faith of two of their five children.

I'm a Failure as a Mother

Eileen's Story

I once felt sure that I had been a bad mother. Two of my five children were not walking with the Lord, and as of the writing of this chapter that remains the case. In addition to this, another child was very troubled for years, due to a physiological ailment, although she is presently immensely better. Please don't get me wrong. I praise God with all my heart for the three who are strong in Jesus Christ, but the fact that our only son is in prison and our daughter is obsessed with making a career in Hollywood has challenged my faith exceedingly! For many days I've agonized over questions like *What happened? Where did I go wrong?*

Like you, I tried so hard to be the best mother I could possibly be. My parents reared me in the fear and nurture of the Lord. I figured if we loved our children, lived Christ in front of them, disciplined them, took them to church twice on the Lord's day and to Sunday school, had family worship regularly, home schooled, enrolled them in a Christian school, protected them from evil influences, read quality literature to them, provided homemade, natural foods and a nice house for them, and gave opportunities for sports and fun activities, then they would turn out as godly, productive citizens. I had the highest hopes that each one of our children would grow up to be on the front lines of Christ's kingdom. But at present, two of these precious gifts from the Lord are not even on the battlefield.

Our son, Paul, has been a jobless, homeless marijuana addict since high school, for eleven years now. Although he made a public profession of faith in Christ at age nine, his claim to faith now vacillates from Christianity to Islam to Rastafarianism, depending on which group is providing his room and board. Having squandered the many athletic and cognitive gifts that God gave to him, he now imagines himself as a profound thinker and professional basketball player. Incarcerated more times than I can keep track of, usually for marijuana possession and probation violations, he views himself as suffering at the hands of a repressive government. One of the most heartbreaking facts of all is that I believe he is incredibly lonely, having barely connected emotionally with anyone throughout his childhood and up to the present.

The other wandering sheep, our daughter Nicole, is the polar opposite of Paul. Also making a public profession of faith at age nine, she seemed to embrace Christ with all her heart. We had no reason to doubt that profession until the last year of university, when she began to express serious doubts about the veracity of Scripture. "I just can't believe that some of my friends, who happen to be homosexuals or non-practicing Jews, are going to hell. They are nicer than many Christians I know." That was five years ago, and since then she has not changed that opinion in the least, although she attends liberal churches sporadically and claims to "have a closer relationship to God than you could ever imagine."

Dear afternoon woman, by now you can understand why I once felt like a failure as a Christian mother. My guess is that some of you are where I once was. You have moments of despondency, depression, and hopelessness. You wonder if God will ever answer your prayers and pleadings for your child. Things only seem to get worse. Your hope grows dimmer and dimmer, until it is barely visible. Just when you see a light at the end of the tunnel, it goes out. I'll never forget the elation I felt when Paul entered boot camp and began to write letters home about how much he remembered the lessons of his boyhood. How much more bitter was the hurt and disappointment when a few weeks later he was discharged from the Marine Corps for using pot after boot camp was over. It seemed that it would have been better not to get my hopes up.

One of my most desperate moments came when our daughter Arielle, at age seventeen, was missing for six days, nowhere to be found. She suffered from neuro-psych Lyme disease, although she had not been diagnosed at that point. Only someone who has experienced something similar can comprehend the panic that goes through a parent's heart. God gave me an immense amount of peace throughout the entire nightmare of Arielle's battles with illness, rebellion, and mental confusion, but it was horrible for all of us nonetheless. Each time she crashed (returned to her violent, self-mutilating behavior after a week or so of calmness) my heart would cry out, *When, Lord, will this end? We can't take this anymore.*

One Sunday morning after church the feeling of being overwhelmed hit me like a tidal wave. Three of my five children were in major spiritual crises at the same time. If it weren't for the faithful prayer and support of my church family as well as my biological family, I know I would have lost my mind. There were times when I couldn't think even one clear thought; I had become so muddleheaded. One Sunday afternoon, twenty people responded to my invitation to join us at our home for prayer and fasting. It was God's provision of biblically thinking, compassionate brothers and sisters that kept me sane and functional.

Another heart-wrenching experience was Paul's first phone call from the holding tank at the county jail. Knowing that we would not bail him out, he appeared to simply want to hear my voice. I still break into sobs when I think about it. Sometimes I'll have a dream in which he is calling out to me, "Momma, Momma." Little lost lambs are especially hard on us mothers because we are often the nurturers in our homes. I'm not saying that the fathers are not deeply hurt, but they tend to be less emotionally expressive than we are.

I suppose the only points more wretched than this one were the days that Paul and Nicole were excommunicated from our church (once it fell on Mother's Day). Even though my husband and I had requested that church elders not delay too long in carrying out church discipline, it was nevertheless an incredibly humiliating and heart-tearing experience. Again, the body of Christ held me up before our Father in heaven, giving me the faith and strength to go on.

The picture I have painted thus far has been dismal indeed, although I am very aware of worse stories than mine out there (but they usually are not in families with such a strong Christian background). I want you to have undeniably clear in your mind that what you are facing with your adult child is not uncommon.

God has chosen a goodly number of his saints to suffer under this burden. I could list respected, godly families in the present generation that have had rebellious children who didn't return to the Lord for decades. Franklin Graham is the most well-known example of this. In Tom Bisset's *Why Christian Kids Leave the Faith*,[1] he claims that research demonstrates that 90 percent of all prodigals come back to live dynamic Christian lives. Whether that statistic is accurate or not, our trust must be in a sovereign God who makes no mistakes.

We see in God's Word that Adam and Eve had their Cain, Aaron had Nadab and Abihu, Noah had Ham, Eli's sons were wicked, Isaac had his Esau, Samuel's sons were lawbreakers, David had Absolom, and the list doesn't end there. Most of these parents are considered to be godly people, but their adult children came to a heartbreaking end.

However, the encouraging stories of godly parents rearing godly offspring abound all the more. For every one of the seeming failures above, Scripture shows us God's grace in each of these families. Remember that Adam and Eve had two godly sons, Abel and Seth; Noah had Shem and Japheth, Abraham had his Isaac, Isaac had Jacob, and Jacob had Joseph. In the lives of Aaron and Samuel, David and Solomon, Eunice and Lois, God's grace is poured out in the lives of children.

Some of the believers I mentioned above, although reared by covenant-keeping parents, sinned grievously at some point in their lives; yet they were renewed to the covenant by the time their lives were ended.

As you consider the lists above, you will see that in a few instances rebels and disciples came from the same set of parents. No doubt some of my readers are thinking about how very different each of their children are. Some who were compliant growing up walk away from Christ during adulthood and, as I mentioned earlier, some who were defiant embrace the faith wholeheartedly many years later.

Below I've listed several biblical principles that I hope will help keep you focused during these heartbreaking years.

Focus on your job, while totally trusting God to do his.

Don't try to do God's job for him. Don't try to do your children's job for them. Remember: God is totally sovereign (Phil. 1:29). God opens and closes hearts (1 Kings 8:58; Ezek. 36:26; Acts 16:4). He does whatever he pleases (Ps. 135:6; Jer. 10:23). Only the Holy Spirit can give the gift of true faith to your children, whether young or grown-up. How often my husband used to pray, "Lord, forgive me for trying to play the role of the Holy Spirit in my child's heart." Being a good parent doesn't instill true faith in Christ in the hearts of our sons and daughters. Such a simple truth is so difficult to learn. Remember: *God has no grandchildren.*

Our job is to pray hard and trust God for the results. I've found that praying in faith is much harder than running around "doing" for our children. We mothers are especially prone to fixing our children's problems, aren't we? From applying bandages to bloody knees to making sure they haven't forgotten their schoolwork, we believe that if they're in a crisis, we are required to immediately come to the rescue.

For some of us, our prayer needs to be, "Lord, let me trust you enough to take my hands off, and let him learn to do this without me." We aren't doing our children any favors if we do for them what they can do for themselves. In fact, we're only creating dependency on ourselves. Our job is to point them to Christ, while helping in age-appropriate ways. Just as a plant can be overwatered, so our offspring can be over-mothered.

As a biblical counselor, I have seen many mothers of adult children who seem driven to make sure their dear child is fed, warm, happy, clean, and socially acceptable.

They seem to be unable to let go. Their whole identity is wrapped up in their children; they become the mothers' purpose for living. These mothers need to be needed, and sometimes they make an idol of their child's love or success. The world calls this enabling behavior or co-dependency; but I think a better word be co-idolatry. The good news about calling some action sin, when it really is sin, is that it can be repented of and forgiven. Praise God for his boundless grace!

Take personal responsibility.

Don't play the shame game or the blame game. Let me encourage you not to take on more or less responsibility than is biblically required. There is no doubt that we, as parents, are 100 percent responsible for our own thoughts, words, and deeds. But it is also true that our children are 100 percent responsible for their own thoughts, words, and deeds. In light of the truth that many Scriptures admonish parents as well as children, it is clear that parents have a huge influence on their children. At the same time, God does not permit any adult or child to blame their sin on their parents.

One of my most vivid memories of dealing with this concept was when our daughter Arielle was very sick with her brain disorder. She had taken one of her many walks, from which she would return, or be returned by the police, hours or days later. Not having been diagnosed as yet, she knew only that she was feeling very angry and agitated and wanted to get out of the house and away from her parents. On this one occasion, she was about fifteen years old and had been missing all night. Because this had happened several times before, I was able not to be totally frantic. I was familiar with the routine by then. At 6:30 in the morning I responded to a call from the police saying that our daughter had been found. When I arrived at the location several miles from our home, the policeman said she had been discovered sleeping on the doorstep of an insurance agent in a dangerous neighborhood. The owner had called the police. The strain must have been obvious by my facial expression, because the man who owned the business and had called the police came to the door and said to me, "This is not your fault. You are not a bad mother." I knew he had hit a nerve in me, because I could hardly keep myself from breaking out in sobs.

For the longest time I had a running argument with myself. If God tells us how to raise our children, and they turn out bad, then isn't that my fault? This is what I call the shame game. Later came the blame game. I'd fall into the ditch on the other side of the road by saying, "This is God's fault. If there is a god, he's cruel or weak." I'd go back and forth between beating myself up for not being able to help my miserable and tortured daughter and being angry and frustrated with her uncontrollable behavior. I'd feel sorry for her; then I'd have a big pity party for myself. Doubts and fears overwhelmed me sometimes. Then God would bring someone into my life just at the right moment to remind me of his promises.

Trust the promises of God. He knows what you need.

Although Romans 8:28 is sometimes overused or misused, it is still one of the most precious promises in all the Word of God, "And we know that in all things God works for the good of those who love him, who have been called according to his purpose" (NIV). The bottom line that we parents of wandering and rebellious children must hold onto constantly is this promise: God knows what I need to become more like Christ. My heavenly Father designed this wretched trial because he loves me and wants me to trust him more, to comfort others who suffer in the same way, and to obey him more eagerly and quickly. The question that has to be answered at the end of the day is, *Do I really believe that God knows what I need and is doing whatever it takes to get the message across to me?* I take great comfort in the knowledge that God is causing this truth to be real in all of his children's lives.

The famous English author C. S. Lewis has written that God whispers to us in our pleasure, speaks to us in our work, but shouts to us in our pain. I've heard much from the Lord as he has instructed me during this painful season in my life.

God will give you the desires of your heart.

Although God has never promised to save each and every one of his children's offspring, he has promised to give you the desires of your heart if you delight yourself in him (Ps. 37:4). Make it your heart's desire that your children know, fear, love, and serve the triune God of the Bible. If that is more important to you than your child's personal appearance, intelligence, career, athletic prowess, acting ability, or emotional happiness, then you can trust that God will give you the desires of your heart.

One more verse that is meaningful to many mothers is Proverbs 22:6, "Train up a child in the way he should go, and when he is old he will not depart from it" (NKJV).

Certainly this promise has kept many distraught Christian parents from losing hope. But there is also a reverse side of this verse. Jay Adams, biblical language scholar, says that it has been poorly translated. Most versions translate the end of the verse "in the way he should go." Adams says that a better translation is "in his own way." In light of this truth, the verse serves as a warning as well as a comfort. The point Solomon is making is that if parents consistently allow a child to choose his or her own way, that will stay with him or her throughout life. A child who has been reared with permissiveness is likely to struggle with submission to authority. One who has been told that God's way is higher than his or her way will more likely learn compliance. My mother often said, "Let her have her own way, and she'll turn out the wrong way."

Never Give Up

To conclude this chapter, let me remind you: *never give up hope.* You can have perfect peace in the midst of the storm. Because the Lord Jesus is bearing our burdens, we can rest knowing that his yoke is easy and his burden is light (Matt. 11:29–30). During the dark hours when you're tempted to give up and feel most overwhelmed, turn your eyes and gaze upon your Savior. The one who made Peter walk on water can keep you from sinking too. I know that's true because he has surely done that for me many times.

During the time when you're waiting for God's salvation, keep praying for and reaching out to your lost son or daughter. We keep writing to our son in prison even though he doesn't respond. Even if your son or daughter has been excommunicated, as two of mine have, you can still speak to them or write to them of Christ's free offer of the gospel. Matthew 18:15–17 teaches us to treat those who have been put out of the church as a pagan or an unbeliever. But these dear pagans need to hear the gospel, no matter how many times they have rejected it. God eventually hardens hearts that repeatedly defy him (Josh. 11:20; 2 Thess. 2:10–11), but when that hardening occurs hasn't been revealed to us. It's not our decision; it's God's. Our job is to keep "speaking the truth in love" (Eph. 4:15), believing that today might be the day of their salvation.

You can also look for natural opportunities to present the claims of Jesus to specific situations your children are facing, while at the same time refusing to compromise your commitments to the Word of God. When there are visits between you, don't change your behavior to suit them. The message that needs to get across to them is that your relationship with God is far more important than your relationship to any family member. I don't claim to walk this narrow road called grace and truth very well. But I thank God that his grace is greater than all my sin.

We cannot outlove God. If we love these wandering souls as much as we do, how much more does our heavenly Father love them? Infinitely more!

1. In what ways were you encouraged by Eileen's story?

2. How did her insights challenge you?

3. In what ways, if any, have you been hanging onto your adult children? How much of your value as a mother or a woman is wrapped up in their success or failure?

4. Is your children's spiritual state the most important concern you have, or are you more concerned about their comfort and health? Although their health and comfort are important issues, they are nothing compared with their ultimate destination.

5. Summarize the teaching of this chapter in four or five sentences.

nine

Here, Mom, Don't Forget Your Sweater

When Jesus then saw His mother, and the disciple
whom He loved standing nearby, He said to His
mother, "Woman, behold, your son!"
(John 19:26)

n the midst of my writing this book, the Lord has brought me through circumstances that expanded my knowledge of caring for elderly members of my family. Previously, my wisdom in this area was primarily academic, something that I had talked to others about and had investigated but had never experienced firsthand. All that has changed now.

Our beautiful tree glowed with luminescent beauty. The crystal, gold, and burgundy ornaments shimmered as the pine-scented fragrance filled our home. The presents were carefully wrapped and spread under the tree. Everything was ready, but Aunt Marion was missing. On Christmas Eve our dear great-aunt suffered a severe stroke that left her almost completely incapacitated and unaware of her surroundings. All the trimmings were as they should have been, but this year our Christmas celebration was different. It was lacking. As our family gathered together on that Christmas day, we were celebrating a birth, but we were also living in the shadow of an impending death. A family member wasn't with us and most probably would never be with us again. Because Aunt Marion had never married, our home and extended family had become her immediate family. She had been a fixture in our family circle, attending every birthday and holiday celebration since her retirement thirty years ago. We missed her on that day—we miss her even more now.

Soon after her stroke, she was placed on hospice care. These kind nurses would come into her home and attend to her, monitoring the swift approach of an unwelcome guest. Twice a week they came in, bathing her, observing her vital signs, and instructing her twenty-four-hour caregivers. We learned that hospice care signaled that the end was near: she had less than six months to live. Our goal in her care changed with the arrival of the hospice team, from that of hoped-for improvement to accepting maintenance. Our concern was that she be made as comfortable as possible and that our hearts, and hers, would be prepared for the inevitable.

Toward the end of February, her condition worsened. She no longer had periods of lucidity but was almost entirely lost in her private thoughts. She spent hours speaking to family members who had passed away before her, laughing and carrying on conversations with the unseen. "They want me to go with them," she told my mother, "but I know enough not to leave until it's time." She sang to God and prayed and was visited by her pastor. He sang, "It Is Well with My Soul" to her, and she asked him to sing it again. We believed that the Lord was working in her soul, graciously fitting her for heaven and loosing her from the bonds of earth.

As my mother was absorbed with overseeing her care, I took upon myself the arrangements for her funeral. I went to the mortuary we had chosen and met with a funeral director. Choices were made. Her personal information was recorded. I composed a letter that would be sent to all of her family and acquaintances, and I put together a mailing list. I helped my mother, who was the executor of her estate and held power of attorney, make decisions. We were trying to prepare ourselves and our family.

At the beginning of March, the hospice team encouraged my mother to remove the feeding tube that had been sustaining Aunt Marion. "Do you think that this is the right thing to do?" she asked the hospice charge nurse. "We're only continuing this feeding for you," she gently explained. My mother and I made the decision, the feeding tube was removed, and the days became even more focused on events in her home.

One evening, shortly before her death, I decided to drop by her house, just to check on her. To my horror, I discovered her caregiver had her boyfriend over and was in bed with him. This unthinkable act was merely the last in a series of disappointments (such as theft of my aunt's belongings) we had encountered with some, though not all, of these women. Needless to say, we relieved her that night and arranged for another nurse to come in. From that time on, we would drop in unexpectedly and watch over my aunt's care conscientiously.

On March 8, at 1:15 A.M., the Lord took our aunt to be with him. In the middle of the night I drove down to her house to join my mother and a faithful caregiver who had been with her for more than three years. I walked into the bedroom that had become her world. There she lay, looking to my eyes just as she had looked for days. I watched her, waiting for her to take a breath; she was still. I held her hand. It was cold. I brushed back her hair and sat down by the side of her bed. I hugged my mother, and we prayed together. The Marion we loved was gone from us, although her body remained. It was time to take care of that temporal home, what Paul called our "earthly tent."

Because Aunt Marion had been on hospice care, we didn't need to have the coroner take her body to the morgue. Instead we called the hospice service, who dispatched a nurse. When she arrived, she checked Marion's vital signs, recorded the time of death, disposed of Marion's medications, called the coroner and the mortuary, and asked us if we would like her to pray with us. Having each of these necessary but daunting arrangements handled by someone familiar with the process was a true comfort.

My mother and I went to the living room and waited for the arrival of representatives from the mortuary. We talked about Marion's life and our assurance that she was resting in the arms of her Savior. The doorbell rang and, after a short discussion and the answering of questions, the mortuary workers rolled in a gurney. "You should probably stay out here, in the living room," they recommended. We complied. After a few moments, they reappeared, this time with the empty gurney filled with the body of our aunt, covered with a green velvet cloth. I watched them wheel her out of her front door, a door she would never cross again, a door she had graced with her presence for more than three decades. The door closed, and I heard the van leave. We would not see her body again until her funeral, five days later. She was gone.

The passing away of someone near is a surprisingly complicated and stressful time. It isn't merely stressful because of the grief that we experience; it is stressful because we have so much to do, so many decisions to make.

God was kind to us in giving us time to prepare. The thought of having to make preparations in the midst of our grief is staggering. At the end of this chapter, I've included a checklist of people to contact and arrangements that you'll need to make when the time arrives. I've also included a list of verses that you might find helpful.

What follows is the experience of my dear friend Karen as she walked through her mother's death. I wanted her to have the opportunity to share this experience with you, so that you will know what may be ahead or be comforted that what you're feeling right now is normal.

Caregiver and Caretaker

Karen's Story

My relationship with my mother had always been a pretty traditional one. My mother was always in the role of the caregiver and nurturer, and I was the child in the role of care "taker" and nurtured. I could always count on my mother to be there when I was in need. She was there to show love, model proper behavior, give guidance, direction, and advice, and show support and encouragement as one who had already walked the many paths of life.

In my mid-thirties this relationship changed. It was a change I was not prepared for or had even given much thought to. I assumed it would come much later on in my life. At that time my life was overly full, and I found myself wearing several hats in my day-to-day routine. As a wife, I was the central cog in a family that was being pieced back together as we had recently gone through a life-threatening car accident with our youngest son. This presented numerous challenges on a daily basis then and for many years to come. As a home-schooling mother of three pre-adolescent boys, my time was fully involved in learning, teaching, scheduling, and chauffeuring. As a homemaker/homeowner of a few homes in the fixer-upper category, I found myself in the middle of numerous unfinished projects of painting, repairing, and remodeling. I was bookkeeper/secretary/owner in a fledgling service business with my husband. The business was providing less than adequate income, and I found myself learning as I went along. I was trying to keep up with clients and vendors, trying desperately to make ends meet, trying to make decisions that would have important consequences, and trying to cope with the pressure that brings. Additionally, I was a fully involved church member in leadership, with others looking to me for my time, answers, and help. I found my life too full with too many weights and circumstances, and I lived with the assumption that just around the corner things would ease up and settle down.

It was into this atmosphere I took a call from my mother that would usher in the change in our relationship. My mother asked me to come to her house, a ninety-minute drive away. There she shared with me her developing estrangement with my father, who was being unfaithful, along with a few more issues. Even though I had spent some time with people with life problems, I was taken aback as to what was happening. I could almost physically feel the shift in the relationship. My mother was now looking to me for care and emotional support and possible answers. I was ill-equipped for this task. I was to learn more in the coming years of my inadequacy in the role of caregiver to my mother, who was becoming the care "taker" in our relationship.

In the next years, my mother experienced several monumental changes in her once-settled life. Her health was deteriorating. Her thirty-four-year marriage dissolved in divorce; she relocated from her longtime home and had to sift through and divide the many years of accumulated material goods and memories. She experienced changes and loss of many friendships with other married couples. She also experienced the ultimate betrayal of her husband as he remarried. Gradually she lost an extremely independent and self-sufficient lifestyle.

As my mother went through these changes, she was drawing closer to me and my family physically by her moving closer to us, and emotionally by her increased confidences. We were now becoming fully involved in her life. As my mother's life began to intertwine with mine on a more intense level, I continued to grow in my new role as caregiver. My mother was losing her life as she had known it, and I was there to bring her into my whirlwind life and family. As my mother's life circumstances were changing, her health steadily eroded. I found myself adding doctor and hospital appointments and consultations into my schedule. Since I did not know what was in the future and did not know how seriously ill my mother was, I responded by thinking that this was a temporary phase, and life would soon go back to a type of normalcy with my mother adjusting to her new life and living closer to me.

Instead I found my level of involvement with my mother growing from twice-weekly visits to her home in a nearby community to eventually moving her into my home to enable me to provide full-time care to her as she became a bed-ridden, dying patient. This was a gradual process that spanned four years. This process included many surgeries and moves in and out of health facilities, hospitals, her home, and my home. My mother's independence continued to deteriorate, until she found herself completely dependent on me and living full-time with my family in our home. About three-quarters of the way through this four-year period I realized that my mother was going to die, and I needed to prepare for that certainty and look to caring for her in the context of a terminally ill person.

Through this four-year process of major life change, my mother and I found that we were to face many challenges in many areas. I have tried to list and address them briefly here. (I can only really explain my side of the relationship with my somewhat limited understanding.)

Time constraint. Perhaps one of the more weighty challenges and the one to which many others relate is the great pressure that only twenty-four hours in one day affords. As the added life chores began to accumulate with my mother, other things were crowded out. The more ill my mother became, the more time-consuming were the chores. Her care situation evolved in the reverse of what caring for my children had been. Rather than finding more time for oneself as the children grow older, the time was lost with her growing dependence. (If one could go backward in time with an adult child and remember how much attention they required at the different developmental stages of their lives until you reached the labor-intensive stage of caring for an infant child, one could get a sense of how the time was gradually lost.) Along with the physical care, there was the time needed and used for the business of life. Bill paying, appointment keeping, supply ordering, and many other mundane chores consumed my time. In the life of a family caregiver, these are chores added into an already full schedule.

Decision making. As my mother became increasingly incapable of making her own decisions, that task fell to me on a daily basis. Not having knowledge of the future or even an assumption of what the future might hold greatly affects the way one decides things. The smaller decisions could be taken in stride: should I move my mother to my home; what should I do with her home; keep her car or sell it. The larger decisions were not so easily dealt with. Would I need to obtain a power of attorney? Should more surgeries and procedures be attempted? What about a "do not resuscitate" order during hospitalizations? Doctors and family looked to me for answers to these questions, and I wasn't sure that I was the one that should be answering the questions, let alone giving the right answers.

Role change. As my mother's circumstances weakened, our relational roles began to change. I was taking the role of the mother and she the role of the child. The shifting of roles vacillated constantly and didn't become permanent until near the end of my mother's life. There was an underlying and constant subtle power struggle going on, with neither of us wanting the change. I have always found the questions of how hard to push, when to encourage, and when to leave alone especially challenging, so it was difficult relating to my mother in the role as a sometime disciplinarian during the times her resolve to do something she needed to do would falter. My constant internal question was, *Where/what is my proper place/behavior?*

Finances. It was easy at the beginning to pay my mother's bills with her funds, but as our lives became more entwined, the question of finances presented a further challenge. My mother was financially solvent and did not have to look to us for support. To add that kind of financial pressure to our already difficult financial situation would have further complicated things. My mother fully trusted me with all she had, but my life experiences hadn't as yet provided me with the maturity I needed to function in that arena. I was learning as I went along. Even though my mother was fully insured medically, it was my desire to care for her myself instead of finding a full-care facility for her. As her care became more intensive, my income-making potential became limited. Was I to charge my mother for my services? Not knowing the future, was I to conserve her funds for a time when her life returned to normal? Being responsible to make financial decisions was a burden I would have gladly given away. As I have two brothers, I realized my fiduciary responsibilities also included them. They were supportive of my actions and trusted me.

Sibling responsibility. I am the youngest of three siblings and the only daughter. I could understand my mother turning to her only daughter during this time in her life, as women are more given to the nurturing parts of life and her bond with me was possibly found in our shared or similar life experiences. This added a new challenge to my life—the challenge of relating anew to two brothers. Our correspondence in the past had not been especially close because we lived in different areas. There was a growing distance that comes with time and noninvolvement with each other. Our mother had been the relationship tender in our family, and when she fell ill we found ourselves working these issues out on our own. At times the added phone calls and information sharing would become a little burdensome, and my wish was that my brothers could know what to do instead of asking me what they should do. At times I felt like I was everyone's caregiver. My brothers were more than willing to do *anything;* the only problem and challenge was being looked to as the orchestrator of all that was happening.

Care "taker" family and friends. As with the sibling challenge, I found myself in the same role with my mother's friends, siblings, and her mother. They would call and want to know what they could or should do, and I was not too helpful because I did not know what to tell them. They were so helpful in providing cards, flowers, and phone calls, and as I wanted to preserve as many of my mother's connections to her life as I could, I felt the weight of keeping these channels open. At the beginning, my mother could carry on her own correspondence, but soon her eyes weren't functioning at full capacity and her mind would slip. That meant these channels gradually closed, as I could not keep up her relationships with people I barely knew. Her isolation was gradual and painful to watch. In making decisions, I had to keep our family and her friends in mind and consider their feelings as well as my own.

Powerlessness. The feelings of helplessness were overwhelming at times. To watch as a once physically vibrant and socially connected woman slid down to the place of almost total isolation was extremely sad. The decline was gradual, as was my acceptance, as the reality of our (mine and my mother's) situation became clear. Seeing the pain and knowing nothing I could do would change it was sobering and painful for me. Trying to fill her life using my own seemed to be so feeble. My grief of knowing I was to lose my mother and knowing there was nothing I could do compounded the helplessness and isolation I felt.

Personal. With only so many hours in each day and the need of time to nurture relationships, my personal relationships suffered. I was emotionally depleted and found myself with little to give as a wife, mother, or friend. In an attempt to provide a nicer and more pleasant environment for my mother during her remaining time, my family moved out of our neighborhood. We relocated thirty miles closer to our business, and we changed churches. Of course this move eliminated some strong support links in our lives, and we all struggled to adjust. As this was a critical time in my three sons' development (adolescence), the pressure to be everything to everyone was immense. My sons used this time to draw away from me and establish themselves as independent young men acting out in ways that one finds common in those years.

They still speak of this time in their lives as when their parents were not around much for them. As my friends tried to help me, I had to answer their offers of help with negative responses because I couldn't express my needs to them. I soon withdrew; I couldn't quite relate to their somewhat normal world since I felt I was in the "valley of the shadow of death." With a strong sixteen-year marriage, I knew our relationship would weather this storm. The difficult part was not having the emotional help from my husband, since he did not really understand the depth of my burden and loss. He was willing but possibly not able to help in this area.

Spiritual. Like my relationships with those around me, my relationship with the Lord became distant also. Having given up my spiritual disciplines of prayer and Bible reading, I resorted to crying out to my God in times of extreme distress. I was able to attend church on a semiregular basis but had to establish new relationships in the new church and used my church time in that pursuit. I found I could not and did not keep a sustained relationship but knew my God was with me as I walked this dark road. My mother had always had a knowledge of the Lord, but I wasn't sure she enjoyed a personal connection with him. Through these years of loss she found God and spent much precious time with him before he took her home.

Living without her. My last challenge, and the one I still find in my life, is the challenge of living life without my mother. The demands on my time did not immediately cease with my mother's death. The funeral decisions, the dissolution of sentimental and personal items, the myriad processes of financial matters, and the devastating grieving process took many, many months to resolve. Eventually I became emotionally numb as I traversed these roads, until I was simply going through the motions. The toll on family relationships took many years to mend.

As I look back on my caregiving experience with my mother, I am truly grateful to the Lord for it. I was able to draw closer to my mother before her death and show love to her in a way she would not have known otherwise. My hope is in him and his goodness, and I rejoice in the hope of life for my mother and myself now and forever.

Below you'll find a list of what you'll need to know if you become responsible for an ailing or dying family member. If you're in the middle of a difficult situation, some of these questions will have already been answered. If you're not there yet, please take time to find out the answers to these questions now, while it's still relatively easy.

- Is there a will? Who is the executor? Where is the will kept?
- Is there an insurance policy? With whom? Who is the beneficiary?
- Has an advanced medical directive been drawn up? Who has the power of attorney for health care? What are your loved one's wishes concerning life-prolonging procedures? Who will make medical decisions for your parents if they are incapacitated?
- Who is your parents' physician? What medications are they on?
- Have you discussed long-term care with your parents and siblings? What are your parents' preferences? Who

will be responsible to make the decision about their care if they are stricken with a chronic debilitating illness?

- Have your parents made any arrangements with a mortuary? Even though this might seem morose, having recorded one's choices before a time of grief will be a loving gift a parent can leave for children.

- Have your parents made arrangements with a cemetery? Where is that information?

- Aside from official agencies, who will need to be notified of your parent's death? Do you know where their addresses are?

- To whom do your parents owe money? What is the general state of their affairs?

1. Have you taken time to ask your parents questions like the ones above? What is stopping you?

2. Have you taken time to speak with your husband and/or children about the above? What is stopping you?

3. Do you have a will?

4. What frightens you most about this topic? What is the biblical view of death? How can you prepare for this eventuality?

5. Ponder these verses about death: Deuteronomy 32:29; Psalms 39:4, 90:12; Luke 12:35–37; 2 Peter 1:14; 2 Corinthians 5:2, 8; Romans 14:8; Philippians 1:20–23. What have you learned?

6. Summarize what you've learned in three or four sentences.

ten

I'm Getting Comfortable with Looking Comfortable

Charm is deceitful and beauty is vain, but a woman who fears the LORD, she shall be praised.
(Prov. 31:30)

'm developing a new self-image: it's the image of an easy chair. I see my lap and my arms as purveyors of comfort and warmth that encompass little children while I read to them. "Come up on Mimi's lap," I invite. "Let's read this book together." Up my little darlings climb. They snuggle in. "Let's read this nice story, shall we?" I ask, and we all find comfort together. Ah, a little bit of heaven on earth.

During the past few years, since around the time I turned forty-five, I began to notice some not-too-subtle changes in my body. These changes began with perimenopause symptoms, including intermittent menstrual periods and hot flashes and ended with my feeling like PMS had become my new permanent boarder. After my hysterectomy, I started hormone replacement therapy (HRT), and I immediately gained fifteen pounds that I haven't been able to lose. I'm looking more and more like my paternal grandmother every day.

Some of these changes are unsettling. I don't like looking in the mirror and seeing cellulite, jowls, and wrinkles. My hands are becoming furrowed, my eyelids are drooping, and the color seems to be fading from my body. I think that this is called the aging process.

In this chapter, I'll begin by describing my journey through this aging process from a personal and a medical perspective. We'll hear from another afternoon friend who'll share her experience with us, and then we'll wrap up our time together with another look at the valiant woman of Proverbs 31.

Menopause Comes Knocking

Understanding what is happening in your body during these years can be helpful. It's nice to know that we aren't all that different from other women and that we aren't going crazy.

Our forties and fifties are not usually the times of our lives when we slow down. In fact, many women find themselves becoming busier during these years, even if the kids have changed their home address. Many women return to college or the work force; others offer daycare for their grandchildren. Still others are consumed with caring for aging or seriously ill parents. And then, in the middle of all of this, we discover strange symptoms plaguing us: insomnia, night sweats, headaches, and disturbing memory loss. Are these symptoms of something seriously wrong with our bodies, or are they a by-product of the stress that we live under?

I first experienced perimenopause (the three to six years before our last period) when I was writing *Women Helping Women* at the age of forty-six. It was a time of high-level stress for me, and I was getting headaches and experiencing memory loss and fuzzy thinking on a scale that was unknown to me before that time. I thought, *I must be going crazy!* So I went to my physician, and she ordered an MRI to see what was going on in my head. The results? There was nothing observably wrong with my brain.

After some investigation, I suggested to her that she run a FSH (follicle stimulating hormone) test to determine whether my ovaries were slowing down the production of estrogen. These changes in hormone levels usually mark the beginning of menopause.

"You're too young," she replied.

"Please, just humor me, will you?" I asked.

It wasn't long until I heard back from her. "You're definitely perimenopausal," she said.

"Great," I said.

I can remember the day that I received that phone call and even where I was standing when my physician told me that life had changed. Could it be that my youth was over? It had gone by so quickly! I remember calling a friend in dismay. "The doctor said that I'm starting menopause," I lamented, feeling as though my life was slipping through my fingers.

"Oh, well, you'll be okay," was my friend's reply.

I was looking for some sympathy. I wanted someone to commiserate with me, but she told me that everything would be all right and that I needed to get on with it! *Thanks a bunch,* I thought. Following my M.D.'s instructions, I scheduled an appointment with my OB-GYN.

"You need to start on hormone replacement therapy," he said.

"But I don't really want to do that yet," I protested.

"Well, these symptoms will probably just get worse, so I'll write out this prescription and then you can get these medications when you decide you want to."

And thus began a five-year-journey that eventually ended with my having a hysterectomy. I struggled through months of intermittent bleeding, bloating, hot flashes, mood swings, and lightheadedness. Menstrual bleeding, which had historically been fairly predictable for me, became utterly erratic. I remember wearing white jeans to a baseball game and . . . well, you know the end to that story.

Along with all this inconvenience and discomfort, I began to develop fibroid tumors that grew quite large and eventually interfered with urination. It was at that time, when I had finally given up trying to handle these problems, that I consented to having a hysterectomy. This isn't an unusual outcome. In fact, about 35 percent of women aged forty-five to sixty-five have hysterectomies.[1]

What to Expect When You'll Never Be Expecting . . . Again

There are a number of ways that you can respond to the onset of menopause. If you find that your symptoms are fairly mild, then there's no reason why you should do anything. However, even though you may be symptom-free, you'll still want to talk with your doctor about combating osteoporosis, the weakening of the bones that occurs after menopause. For this, you could take a calcium tablet, or, if you have trouble digesting them, pop a few antacid tablets—you probably need them anyway! For those of you who have some of the other symptoms, you might try to control your experience of them by being sure to eat properly, avoiding caffeine, and getting plenty of regular exercise. These three steps will be the most important ones you can take, no matter how you handle the rest of this process. Other women will find relief by using herbs or more homeopathic substances.[2]

There will also be some women whose symptoms are more severe and wide-ranging, and they will consider hormone replacement therapy. Generally, HRT consists of the intake of two primary hormones: estrogen, usually in the form of Premarin or a generic and progesterone. Women who still have their uterus will usually take both hormones, while women who have had a hysterectomy will take only estrogen. Dr. Shirley Galucki writes, "There are three main reasons women consider HRT: relief of symptoms associated with menopause (hot flashes, vaginal dryness, mood fluctuations), prevention of osteoporosis, and prevention of cardiac disease."[3]

Recently two important studies have published findings that might influence your decision to take the combination of prescription estrogen and progesterone. The Women's Health Initiative conducted by the National Institute of Health has announced that they are abandoning their study because the risks of other diseases, especially breast cancer, is too high. In May 2003, the National Institute of Health also found that women taking this combination of hormone replacement therapy had "twice the rate of dementia, including Alzheimer's disease, compared with women who did not take the medication."[4] The findings of these two studies strongly suggest that the risks taking the combination of estrogen and progesterone far outweigh the benefits. In light of these facts, you'll want to work closely with your physician to find other relief for your menopausal symptoms. If you no longer have a uterus and are just taking an estrogen replacement, these studies do not apply to you, although you still might want to speak with your physician if you have concerns.

After the Surgery

By the time that I finally arrived in the operating room for my hysterectomy, I was glad. I know that's not how all women feel. I know that many women are troubled about the loss of their uterus and that for some, the changes that this procedure portends are frightening.

Once a friend who had just had a hysterectomy asked me, "Do you miss your uterus?"

"No," I replied, "we were never that close."

For me, the trouble caused by my reproductive organs was taking up too much thought, time, and effort. The discomforts and distresses were overshadowing any thoughts that I might have had about my need for this piece of my anatomy. I know that many women feel strongly about this; I'm not one of them. If the decision to have a hysterectomy comes to a woman before she's finished having children, or if it comes to her at a time in her life when she's going through other difficulties, then it can be disheartening, and I'm not meaning to be glib. What follows is the experience of another valiant afternoon friend, Barbara Lerch.

Barbara's Story   How can I describe the feeling of strangeness and detachment that filled my mind those first weeks and months after my surgery? Rather than the three small incisions I had expected, a discovery during surgery resulted in a long, silvery line of staples. The shocking size of the wound, the unnaturalness of the glistening metal, the doctor's report of how many things had been removed stunned me. I felt bewildered, stilled. When I had courage enough, my fingers lightly explored the altered landscape of my abdomen. Much of it felt the same. But, how could it? So much that had been inside me was now forever altered. The body I had lived with so long now felt alien, unknown, secretive. Several months into my recovery, a painful lump arose in my breast. The following weeks brought new visits to my specialist, and then more surgery. More of my body gone away in jars to the lab. I stood before my mirror, hysterectomy scar still red, one breast stitched and swollen, dark blue and purple. What had happened to me? Was this still my body, or some alien thing bent on destroying me? In the past it had been my comfortable, although quirky, friend. I asked my reflection, "Who am I, now? What am I, now? With so many parts gone, am I still a woman?" What is it that makes a woman womanly? God answered me and led me gradually to see my identity based on his blood, rather than my monthly blood.

I am his child because he bled and died for me. I am a woman because he sculpted my heart and person this way, not because of my reproductive capabilities. And he gave me this body for his glory and purposes, that I might serve him and his people through it, regardless of what happens to it. My body still keeps its secrets from me, but I am learning to live with it in a new way. It has new quirks and demands. I have learned that this funny body will abide with me as long as my Savior wishes.

For all that is new and different, there is something that is not new or different: God's purposes for me and my body. The good works he created for me to do are still out there, awaiting my action. Although my fruitfulness in one area is finished, a kingdom full of other opportunities for fruitfulness is all around me.

So, I am an afternoon woman, and glad of it. It is a good thing not to trust in a firm young body. It is a good thing to know that this body will return to dust. It is a good thing to know that our days are written in his book, yes, every one of them. It is a good thing to live with our whole hearts, to invest our gifts in the kingdom of God and its people, in God's creation. For all that I love on this earth, I must learn over and over to love without demanding permanence from things only of this world. My heart must yearn first for his face, his presence.

This afternoon woman is renewed daily in Christ. I am ready to love, to laugh, to cherish in new ways. I am still running the race described in Hebrews, but now I run with arch supports. Much of the journey of faith still lies ahead. I take a deep breath. I close my eyes and feel the sun on my face. I smile. What will God do today?

As I said, my experience was different. That doesn't mean it was more right. I had less concern about what these changes meant about me. I am a woman if I am infertile, if I am without a uterus or a breast. I am a woman in my chromosomes and most importantly in my soul before a loving heavenly

Father, who created me to be a woman, and nothing can change that.

Wherever you are in this process—beginning to learn new words, or like me, pretty much through it—it is appropriate for you to spend some time thinking, reading, and praying about the new challenges that you're facing. "The best way to be prepared for menopause is to first be educated about the subject. Knowing what to expect can relieve a lot of excess stress which a woman could unnecessarily put on herself if she began noticing . . . symptoms but didn't know what to do."[5]

In the second endnote of this chapter, I've suggested some reading that you could do to follow up on what we've talked about. In any case, remember that changes are part of the way that God has created the world to function, and the change of life isn't a surprise or difficulty for him. He'll use it in your life for his glory and your good, and all you need to do is recognize that menopause isn't the end of life, nor is it a failure to be a woman. It's a new season. I'm happy not to have to buy tampons, struggle with cramping, or live in the shadow of PMS any longer. The new freedom that I'm experiencing is one part of the silver lining that these erstwhile gloomy clouds of menopause can bring.

Managing Your Health

First Corinthians 6:19–20 reads, "Do you not know that your body is a temple of the Holy Spirit who is in you, whom you have from God, and that you are not your own? For you have been bought with a price: therefore glorify God in your body."

Although these verses primarily speak of your responsibility to refrain from sexual immorality, the implications for the care of your body are clear. We, our spirits, souls, and bodies, belong to God. He has purchased us with the precious blood of our Redeemer, and we need to live daily in the light of that gracious reality.

The Westminster Larger Catechism comments on the requirements of the sixth commandment, "Thou shalt not kill," stating that it is our duty to maintain "a sober use of meat, drink, physic,[6] sleep, labor and recreations."[7] I know that I don't generally think that it is a godly responsibility to be sure that I'm caring for my body. My motives normally run more along the lines of feeling good or being able to fit into my clothing. I don't usually contemplate God's claim on my body and his command to be a good steward of the body he's entrusted me with. But God's rule extends even here. I need to ask, *Am I trying to maintain my body in as good health as is possible?* That doesn't mean that it's sinful for me to age or have chronic diseases, although it was sin that first introduced sickness. It means that I need to manage the gifts he's given me—and not squander them through an intemperate misuse or neglect of proper nutrition, rest, exercise, or medical help. I need to be sure that I'm getting enough but not too much sleep, working six days and resting one, and spending adequate time in restful recreations.

Glorify God in Your Body

If you're like most Christians, you probably tend to think that God is more interested in your soul than he is in your body—and in one sense, your eternal life with him, that's true. But in another sense, it's not. Look again at the verse above. Paul tells the Corinthians to "glorify God with their bodies." While we're confined here to this earth, everything that we do, we do in our bodies. We worship and serve God with our body, which houses our soul, and we sin against him in our thoughts and actions, functions of our body. We can glorify God in our body by joyful obedience, or we can live for our own pleasures, whether that encompasses gossip or laziness, gluttony or over-work. Paul wanted his readers to live in such a way that others would know of God's glory—his magnificence and grace—and would be inspired to praise and love him too. He instructed them to glorify God in their body! It's surprising that your care of your body can make a difference to the Lord, but it's obvious that it does.

The Desire for Beauty

Recently a good friend turned forty-two. While I was wishing her a happy birthday, she mentioned her age and reported that another friend said she still looked young. A little bit in jest I told her that really was an insult, biblically speaking. According to the Scriptures, old age is more desirable than youth. Our culture's subconscious assumption that older people are useless is antithetical to all that the Scriptures teach. The following verses on the aged are meant to transform your thoughts from the world's model of youth-worship.

> You shall rise up before the grayheaded and honor the aged, and you shall revere your God; I am the LORD. (Lev. 19:32)

> Wisdom is with aged men, with long life is understanding. (Job 12:12)

> A gray head is a crown of glory; it is found in the way of righteousness. (Prov. 16:31)

The glory of young men is their strength, and the honor of old men is their gray hair. (Prov. 20:29)

For the one whose life has been lived in covenant relationship with God, the Bible assumes that there will be wisdom and honor. Young people do have physical strength and can be wise beyond their years, but older people have the maturity and strength that is produced only in the caldron of faith lived out in this sin-cursed world.

> The woman who has lived out God's counsel through years of toil and trial has resilience, stamina, and a faithful perspective. Godly wisdom supersedes any loss of physical prowess she may be experiencing. Therefore, Paul instructed Titus to raise up mature, godly women to counsel [younger] women.[8]

The Valiant Woman Understands What's Important

As I wrote in chapter 2, the picture of the valiant woman of faith in Proverbs 31 is not one of youth. This woman, the quintessential standard for godliness, is timeless and aged. She's old enough to have lived a life filled with challenge and victory. You've heard from her in many of our chapters. Remember, she's not to see herself as the typical Middle Eastern picture of woman as a man's sex toy. Neither is she the Greek view of woman as merely idle wisdom. The biblical portrait is the *eset hayil,* a term that should be "understood as the female counterpart of the *gibbor hayil,* the title given to the 'mighty men of valour' . . . in David's age."[9] The godly woman of Proverbs 31 is a mighty woman of valor, a warrior who contends fearlessly for her family, her community, and her God.

Proverbs 31 is a portrait in verbs—but not merely action for action's sake. She's wisdom in action.[10]

It isn't surprising that she's not much interested in charm or beauty, is it? How far have you ventured from this perspective of what is worthwhile in a woman?

Building Your House on the Rock

The valiant afternoon woman has focused her life on God's calling. Perhaps she's still a homemaker; or she might be involved in ministry or perhaps in a secular occupation. She might be a grandmother or may still be awaiting grandchildren; perhaps she's single, having never married or having become single through death or divorce. Whatever her marital status or daily employments, she's inwardly beautiful and filled with a wisdom that finds its satisfaction in loving, life-giving service to others.

Instead of focusing on the externals that our culture screams at you about, discipline yourself to think deeply about the internal qualities that God honors. Think about building your house through wisdom and filling it with the precious and pleasant riches that knowledge provides (Prov. 14:1; 24:3–4). Consider how important the wisdom that you have is: wisdom that can be used to teach younger women about the path of life and save the gospel from disgrace (Titus 2:3–5). Refrain from focusing your energies primarily on your outward appearance, seeking instead to be modest, discreet, and filled with the good works that befit a godly woman (1 Tim. 2:9–10). Think about the characteristics that qualified a widow for care and support by the church: fidelity, charity, hospitality, diligence, and benevolence (1 Tim. 5:9–10).

As we come to the end of our time together, ponder anew how three godly men described the valiant afternoon woman: "She must be well thought of by everyone because of the good she has done. Has she brought up her children well? Has she been kind to strangers as well as to other Christians? Has she helped those who are sick and hurt? Is she always ready to show kindness?" (1 Tim. 5:10, TLB).

Peter instructs her in this way: "Don't be concerned about the outward beauty that depends on jewelry, or beautiful clothes, or hair arrangement. Be beautiful inside, in your hearts, with the lasting charm of a gentle and quiet spirit that is so precious to God" (1 Peter 3:3–4, TLB).

And finally, as we began our study, let's return now to King Lemuel and let him remind us that "charm is deceitful and beauty is vain, but a woman who fears the LORD, she shall be praised" (Prov. 31:30).

Do you trust that God's words are true? Do you believe that fearing the Lord is more important than looking young?

Rich and Fruitful Lives from Beginning to End

The Lord has ordered his universe to change, grow, transform, and fade away. He's ordered our lives as women in much the same way. We're changing, growing, and transforming. Segments of our life are fading away, while others are just now being born. In all of this, my beloved sisters, God is lovingly teaching us of himself and causing us to long for the day when all this change will end and we'll glory in his presence, gazing eternally into his blessed face. In the meantime, he's provided us with enough grace and wisdom to live valiantly and reverently. Will you trust him? Will you embrace his plan for you and humbly bow your knee before it? Do you see how good and kind he's been to you? Allow me to personalize Psalm 92 for you, my excellent sister:

> The righteous woman will flourish like the palm tree, she will grow like a cedar in Lebanon. Planted in the house of the LORD, she will flourish in the courts of our God. She will still yield fruit in old age; she shall be full of sap and very green, to declare that the LORD is upright; He is her rock, and there is no unrighteousness in Him!

1. What bothers you the most about growing old?

2. Where are you on the perimenopause/menopause continuum? Have you studied the relevant data that will help you make wise decisions?

3. How are you doing with taking care of your body? Do you see that God has given you a body so that you can glorify him during your earthly journey? What might you need to change?

4. As you think back over the topics we've covered in this chapter, is there any one that you need to revisit and work on?

5. Do you see that God is calling you to a valiant, fruitful life, even in your afternoon years? What is his purpose in doing this? (See Ps. 92:15.) Ponder these verses:

> "O God, you have taught me from my youth,
> And I still declare your wondrous deeds.
> And even when I am old and gray, O God, do not forsake
>   me,
> Until I declare Your strength to this generation,
> Your power to all who are to come." (Ps. 71:17–18)

6. Summarize what you've learned in this chapter.

eleven

Afternoon Women in Ministry

. . . for she herself has also been a helper of many.
(Rom. 16:2)

s we have traversed through our afternoon experiences, we've focused primarily on possible problem areas in our personal lives. We've looked at our differing and varied relationships, primarily in the home, and we've thought about ways to make the most of this season of our lives, taxing as it may be. In this chapter, however, we'll shift our focus from our nearest neighbors (those who live with us) to those in our church and community, and we'll explore the areas of ministry that may be opening to us now.

Although the afternoon of life is a time fraught with great change, it's also frequently a time when priorities can be reevaluated and time can be freed up. After the children move away (and before they move back in again!), if you don't find yourself working at a full-time job, you may find that you've got a little more discretionary time on your hands: time that can be used for the benefit of those outside your immediate family.

Women Who Teach

Part of Paul's counsel to Titus, as he established churches in Crete, was that he should recognize the great resource that was available to him in an often overlooked segment of his congregation. Paul wrote,

> Older women likewise are to be reverent in their behavior, not malicious gossips nor enslaved to much wine, teaching what is good, so that they may encourage the young women to love their husbands, to love their children, to be sensible, pure, workers at home, kind, being subject to their own husbands, so that the word of God will not be dishonored. (Titus 2:3–5)

An older woman, in the afternoon of her life, has gifts and experience to bring to younger women who aren't there yet. In another letter about church order, Paul wrote that women were not to "teach or exercise authority over a man" (1 Tim. 2:12). Although this restriction still applies to women exercising a teaching authority over a man, Paul isn't saying that women aren't to teach anyone. Instead, he tells Titus that older women are to be teaching. Their audience? Younger women. Their topic? How to live godly, sane, sensible lives, and how to do all the things that they've just walked through. (Just as we've done in this book!)

Since there are a number of good books on what's being called the Titus 2 Ministry,[1] I won't attempt to do an exhaustive study of this topic. Instead, I've asked an afternoon friend, Anita Manata, to write her thoughts about women's roles in the church.

Women Ministering to Women in the Church — *Anita's Story*

God has planned wisely for the ministry of all his children in the church. Throughout Scripture we see his emphasis on building interpersonal relationships that reflect his character and encourage mutual growth in godliness. In this way his bride is continually being built up toward the day she will finally be united with him. The individual members of the church use their unique gifts within the framework of their personalities to promote spiritual growth in his bride and to bear witness of him in the world.

But God's wisdom in designing the way the members of his church use their gifts according to their personalities also includes the framework of the particular roles men and women have in ministry in the church. Specifically for women, God's model is found in Titus 2:3–5. It is here that we find whom God has designed for women to minister to in particular: *Women are to minister to women, and older women should instruct younger women in how to be godly in their varied situations.*

It is true that every woman in the church, no matter her age, should be using her gifts to build interpersonal relationships that are mutually edifying. Younger women

179

will have many opportunities to minister to older women according to their gifting as well. Even though this is true, we should pay attention to the pattern that Paul tells Titus to teach in his church. To neglect it is to miss out on the perfect wisdom in God's design.

Hindrances to This Ministry

Age-Specific Groupings

The Titus 2 model, that of older women instructing younger women in godliness, is contrary to everything we see in our fallen culture. From early childhood children are grouped according to their age in schools and even in some Sunday schools. This practice may have some benefit for certain developmental reasons. But the model of age-group peers then becomes the norm even for adults in some Sunday school and care group programs. You have classes for groups such as college and career, the young married, the parents of young children, the parents of teens, and even seniors. Such age grouping inhibits the Titus 2 cross-age relationships from developing. God's wisdom in calling individuals from a wide variety of walks of life is that his church is built up when its members learn from and share in each other's experiences.

God, in his wisdom and kindness, designed women to be relational. He made them nurturers and helpers. By his design it should be natural for older women to help and nurture younger women by encouraging them to develop a godly attitude and focus. As a woman matures in her life and her faith, she naturally has more to offer women with less experience. A woman who is less mature is tempted to be devoted to something other than her family, to be undisciplined, or to be self-focused rather than practicing kindness toward others. But the more mature woman has learned how to fight the fight of her faith in these areas more consistently and so has much to share. Life in the body of Christ is about members supporting and encouraging each other to put on godly attitudes and actions.

Godly, mature women should be conscious of their propensity to gather with other women of their age group, as well. So, even though it might seem that the church is encouraging this kind of separation, we should guard against gravitating to those with whom we are most comfortable, and seek to live sacrificially instead.

Focus on Personal Leisure and Growth

Older women are naturally suited to helping younger women not just because they have had more experience but because they often have more time since their children have grown and left the home, or since some have reached retirement age. Our culture is contrary in this aspect as well. Women in this age group are encouraged to do something to build up their self-image. The thinking is that since they have given so much of their life to helping others, now that they have time, they deserve to spend it on doing what they want to do. Yoga and art classes become popular means for self-fulfillment, as do studies in New Age religious philosophies. Perhaps this error existed in some way in New Testament days, which would explain why Paul tells Titus to instruct older women to be others-focused rather than self-focused. A woman will always find more fulfillment in living biblically than in

181

trying to fulfill herself through popular means. The way to find our life is to lose it.

Even in the church, the Titus 2 model is often not practiced as much as it should be. Some churches have had some success in implementing Bible study groups where some of the more mature women take turns leading the devotionals or studies. Some churches have expanded that model to include having a group of women come to the home of a more mature woman to learn a certain recipe or other home skill. But the practice of Titus 2 relationships among women ought to be happening aside from formal programs too.

Relationships can and should be developed outside of these more formal church programs. For instance, a woman might find a younger woman in her neighborhood or in her congregation whom she will seek to mentor in an informal way, perhaps without even stating that that's what she's seeking to do. The church may or may not need to be involved in this process—having coffee together a couple of times a month and sharing experiences would probably be a great benefit to a young woman. Being available to baby sit or help with overwhelming chores would also demonstrate a heart of Christ-like service.

Sinful Fears

Sometimes the reason that this kind of one-to-one ministry is not happening is due to the sinful fears that keep us from building any of our relationships the way we should. Some older women may assume that it would be impolite for them to start telling younger women how to manage as wives and mothers or how to practice self-control and kindness. They may think that since culture is always changing, and what is common for women today was not when they were the same age, they have nothing pertinent to offer. They may fear that they will give the impression that they are know-it-alls. One thing maturity tends to work in a person's heart is the humility of learning that there is still so much to learn. And so, when they should be in a place to be most useful in the church, they struggle with thinking they are of little or no use.

One way that churches could help overcome this would be to encourage the younger women to invite the older women to instruct them in a variety of ways. They could call for help with problems or invite them over for coffee. A younger woman could build a friendship with an older woman and find out all about her experiences. In doing so, she would be building a resource for future help. Younger women, however, also struggle with worrying that since they are young and do not have the same depth of experience that the older women will find them boring or childish. They also have the demands of a younger family or new career that makes finding the time to build relationships difficult. And so, in some churches the Titus 2 model is rarely put into practice. Even so, even if it is not being formally practiced in your congregation, you can take steps to follow Paul's instructions to establish cross-generational relationships on a less formal, more individual basis. You don't need to wait for the church to institute an official program: you can build relationships with younger women on your own.

Biblical Living Is War

We must remember that living biblically is never easy. It is war. To try to live by what God has said flies in the face of secular culture and our sinful desires. But much of the battle is won in becoming aware of what God would like us to do, and then beginning to fight the fight of faith in that area. Women should be frequently taught and reminded how important it is to build meaningful, encouraging relationships with each other. They need to be especially encouraged to build these relationships outside of their same age peers. Church leaders also have a responsibility to teach the same things Paul told Titus to teach about developing cross-age relationships for the goal of instructing in godly living. If this kind of instruction is coming from the pulpit and from the leaders in the church, it will begin to have an impact on the whole body.

The great benefit of a church that practices the Titus 2 model successfully is that God's Word will not be reviled (Titus 2:5). The world will look at the church and see people living lives that glorify God by practicing his Word. Instead of older women feeling useless, they will be respected and honored in the church. Rather than younger women feeling frustrated and alone in learning about life, they will feel the support and care of the more experienced women. The church will be stronger and healthier as its members minister to each other biblically. What could be a more worthy goal?

Reverent in Behavior

The primary requirement of the afternoon woman who is involved in mentoring or teaching younger women concerns her character. She is to be "reverent" in her behavior. In instructing the women to be reverent, Paul is referring to what he wrote earlier about the older men. Since this reference is the only time this particular Greek word is used, we can get a better picture of what Paul is talking about by looking at the previous verse, where Paul describes the qualities he wants to see in older men. They are to be "sober-minded, dignified, self-controlled, sound in faith, in love, and in steadfastness" (Titus 2:2 ESV). Before you or I can wisely instruct other women, we are to walk into these qualities. Some of the things that we're to teach the younger women are first to be learned and practiced by us.

Being sober-minded. The Greek word is translated "sober-minded" twice and "vigilant" once, and I think that this gives us a clear picture of what Paul is getting at. A godly older woman should abstain from the immoderate use of alcohol or any substance that might cloud her judgment and influence her character, causing her to let down her guard in an ungodly manner.

Dignified. A godly afternoon woman should be known as someone who is honorable and worthy of respect.

Self-controlled. Once again, Paul stresses the necessity of temperance and discretion. The Greek word has a connotation of "curbing one's desires and impulses."[2]

Sound in faith. Women should strive to have doctrine that is free from error and soundly built upon the veracity of the God of the Bible, as he has revealed himself in the Bible.

Sound in love. We don't only need sound doctrine; we also need to be strong in the graces of love for our God and for our neighbor.

Sound in steadfastness. Steadfastness is the characteristic of a woman "who is not swerved from [her] deliberate purpose and [her] loyalty to faith and piety by even the greatest trials and sufferings."[3] We've looked at some of the typical trials a woman experiences in this time of life. Paul would say to us: "If you've stood through these times, you've got something of great value to give to the younger women. Persevere during times of doubt and trouble. Your life is a rich treasure trove of the jewels of wisdom that your younger sisters need."

As Carolyn Mahaney writes in *Feminine Appeal,* "Our conduct has a direct influence on how people think about the gospel. The world doesn't judge us by our theology; the world judges us by our behavior. *They want to see if what we believe makes a difference in our lives.* Our actions either bring honor to God or misrepresent His truth."[4]

Before we look at all other ministry opportunities that are open to us as afternoon women, may I encourage you to review the list above and ask the Lord to grant you the grace to convict and change you in the areas where you're weak? Remember that it's his plan to sanctify you wholly, and all for his glory.

Women Who Teach Children

Aside from teaching younger women, older women are also encouraged to teach children. In fact, women were instrumental teachers of Paul's protégé, Timothy. Paul writes that the faith that he saw in Timothy first dwelt in his grandmother,

Lois, and his mother, Eunice (2 Tim. 1:5). He told Timothy to "continue in the things you have learned and become convinced of, knowing from whom you have learned them and that from childhood you have known the sacred writings which are able to give you the wisdom that leads to salvation through faith which is in Christ Jesus" (2 Tim. 3:14–15).

Timothy had heard the truth about Jehovah and ultimately about Jesus Christ through his mother and grandmother, and probably from Paul during his first missionary journey to Lystra. Even though Paul may have been the direct means that God used for Timothy's salvation, it's plain that Timothy's heart had already been prepared by the good work of his mother and an older woman, Lois. Lois used the wisdom that she had learned to plant truth in the heart of her darling grandson.

Lemuel, the writer of Proverbs 31,[5] says that he learned about the characteristics of a godly woman from his mother. Since the beginning of the family, mothers and grandmothers have been instrumental in teaching truth to their sons and daughters. We don't know how old Lemuel was when his mother taught him how to find a good wife, but it's clear that she had great influence on him. Afternoon women should take every opportunity to teach the children around them, whether in Sunday school classes, backyard Bible clubs, or around the family dinner table.

Women Who Teach Men

Although women are prohibited from teaching men in a formal or authoritative church setting, at least one woman is mentioned teaching a man in a private setting. Priscilla and her husband, Aquila, were a teaching team, and Paul didn't have any trouble with that role for her. Aquila and Priscilla accompanied Paul to Ephesus and stayed there, strengthening the church while he traveled on. In Acts 18:26 we read about the correction that Priscilla and Aquila brought to Apollos: "But when Priscilla and Aquila heard him, they took him aside and explained to him the way of God more accurately" (Acts 18:26). It's not necessary in this chapter to make too much of this verse, but it is appropriate to at least mention the fact that Paul didn't have any problem with this kind of ministry. Remember that the ministry was a private one and was probably done in conjunction with her husband.

Women Who Counsel Women and Men

It is now, and always has been, my position that women are called to counsel other women and to seek to train and encourage them to fulfill a *Women Helping Women* ministry.[6] In my personal counseling ministry I counsel women almost exclusively, although there have been occasions when I have been counseling a wife and had her bring her husband in for updates or to gather more information.

In light of all this though, I don't think that it is sinful or unbiblical for women to give counsel to men; especially in the relationship between husband and wife, I believe that women are called to do so.[7] As Thomas R. Schreiner writes,

> Women, then, have engaged in significant ministries, even if those ministries were unofficial. One thinks of Abigail in 1 Samuel 25. Abigail was not a prophetess and had no other official ministry that we know of. Nevertheless, her humble and gentle advice to David persuaded him not to kill Nabal. *How many*

unrecorded events there must be of women persuading men, humbly and gently, to pursue a more righteous course![8]

Grandmother to the Church

I wasn't saved until my early twenties, and I remember a woman in the church I began attending, whom we knew as Mom Cazier. After my conversion, I immediately started Bible college and, together with others, we would look to Mom Cazier to cook for us and lend a loving hand. I remember her as a humble, diligent woman who wasn't concerned about whether she received the limelight and seemed happy just to take care of the students. She made sure that we had doughnuts at our break, and when it was time to raise some money for the "starving students," she was right there for us. I particularly remember the tacos she made and what a difference her love made to me.

What a delightful testimony it would be to God's grace if every woman reading this book decided to adopt a few of the young people in her church.

Women Who Upbuild, Encourage, Entreat, and Console

Whatever your position is on what prophecy is and whether this gift still might be existing today, it's obvious that Paul didn't have a problem with women bringing a word of upbuilding, encouragement, or consolation to the New Testament church (see 1 Cor. 14:3) or with their praying publicly in the church (1 Cor. 11:5).

When he was giving direction to the Corinthians about church prayer and prophecy, he could have said, "I do not allow a woman to pray or encourage anyone publicly." But

189

that's not what he said. When instructing the Corinthians, he said that husbands and wives could pray and prophesy publicly, although the wife must do so with her head covered, as a sign of the authority she recognizes (1 Cor. 11:5, 10) and of her desire to be recognized as a woman. Although Paul upholds biblical male leadership by not allowing women to judge "prophecies," he does allow them to minister in a prophetic word or in prayer. As Schreiner writes, "Paul affirms that women can prophesy . . . that women have prophetic gifts and he wants them to exercise those gifts in the church, but he does not want them to overturn male leadership."[9]

I realize that many people who are reading this believe that the gift of prophesy had ceased, but even so, perhaps some platform for a mature, godly woman to speak to the congregation in words that would not be characterized as directive, but rather as upbuilding, encouraging, or consoling to the hearers, would be allowed. How this might be finessed, or whether wise older women could speak to the entire congregation in a public setting, or if these words might be delivered in a more private setting, such as a home group or smaller meeting, is to be decided in each individual congregation.

In any case, women prophets were known and recognized in the Old and New Testaments. Deborah was called a prophetess and a judge (Judg. 4:4). She was a woman who was acknowledged as having God's word, and "the people of Israel came up to her for judgment." Huldah, the prophetess, was inquired of by priests and male leaders, even when there were male prophets in Israel, and she delivered the "word of the Lord" to them (2 Kings 22:14–20).

Miriam, Moses' and Aaron's sister, is also called a prophetess (Exod. 15:20–21). She led the women in a dance of worship after the deliverance at the Red Sea. She is also referred to as a leader of the nation of Israel in Micah 6:4: "I brought you up from the land of Egypt and redeemed you from the house of slavery, and I sent before you Moses, Aaron, and Miriam."

In the New Testament, Anna is referred to as a prophetess (Luke 2:36). Matthew Henry writes of her, "Happy the court that had a prophetess within the verge of it, and knew how to value her."[10] These women spoke to men and women for their good, and wise women who have the "word of the Lord" from the Scriptures should be allowed to function in some capacity today, all the while recognizing and embracing male headship in the church and home.

Women of Prayer and Praise

One of the most valuable ministries an afternoon woman can embrace is prayer. Again, Anna, a woman who is much older than an afternoon woman, spent all of her time in the temple, worshiping with fasting and prayer night and day (Luke 2:37). She recognized Jesus as the Messiah and gave thanks to God, speaking of him to all who were waiting for the coming of the Messiah.

When I think of women who pray, I think of my mother-in-law, Thelma. I have heard her say for many years how she had interceded in prayer for her children and grandchildren, frequently spending hours in prayer at night. Even though God sovereignly elects those who will be saved, he also uses means, and I trust that her prayers will be the means of the ultimate salvation of all my children and grandchildren.

Jesus commended the worshipful ministry of Mary of Bethany when she anointed his body before his crucifixion. He said that her offering of compassionate devotion would be

191

memorialized for all church history, granting her expression of praise a great significance. "Truly I say to you," Jesus said, "wherever this gospel is preached in the whole world, what this woman has done will also be spoken of in memory of her" (Matt. 26:13).

Even if we feel that our gifting doesn't lie in other more public arenas, we can all give ourselves to impassioned worship in gratitude for lives lived under his hand of blessing.

Women Who Evangelize

One of my dearest friends, Donna, is an afternoon woman I also refer to as an "attack-dog witnesser." Her heart is full of the love of Christ, and she almost bursts out with testimony of the Lord's grace every opportunity she gets. She has a special burden for young people and longs to see them saved and will frequently spend hours just getting to know them so that she might have an opportunity to share the gospel. Again, I do believe that God sovereignly chooses those who will be saved, but he also uses means, and she's got "means" written all over her.

Afternoon women, sometimes due in part to their age, have an opportunity to speak to others about their faith and the wonderful gospel. I recall my former years when I was more concerned about what people thought of me and how my desire to please people sufficiently silenced my testimony. As I've grown older, I'm not quite so concerned about what anyone else thinks, and I'm particularly not concerned about whether I make a good impression.

Women Who Write

One of the greatest opportunities to help others is through the written word. I'm always humbled, amazed, and blessed when women come to me at conferences and tell me that their lives have been touched by something I've written. It's so surprising to me that God has presently chosen to use me in this way, and I'm so thankful for it, although it doesn't make sense to me.

Think of all the women writers who have blessed you through the years. One woman I really love reading is Andree Seu, who writes for *World* magazine. Whenever I get a new copy of *World,* I always flip to the back to see if she's written something in that issue. I'm challenged by her style and intelligence but most of all by her Christian worldview and insight.

Many other women have been gifted to write, and I remain thankful for their ministry. Just think about how much richer our lives are because Corrie ten Boom recorded her story. Do you have a story that needs recording? In our electronic age, I think we've lost the skills of letter writing. I know that our words can encourage others who are far away, even on the mission field, and are like drinks of cold water to a thirsty soul. Proverbs 25:25 says, "Like cold water to a weary soul, so is good news from a distant land."

Women Who Lead Women

Because of God's grace in my life, I have the wonderful privilege of traveling around the country speaking to women's groups in different churches. A natural outgrowth of that is that I usually get to have a time of fellowship and prayer with women who are leading other women. What a blessing that is! Most of these women are afternoon women, and they love God and have a great burden for other women.

So Many Opportunities, So Little Time

Because of time and space restrictions, I can't speak more about all the wonderful ministries that are open to afternoon women. I can think of women who write and have encouraged me, of women who compose worship songs or design beautiful art. Women should also function in mercy ministries, like Phoebe and Dorcas did in the New Testament.

The world in general and the church in particular are filled with hurting people. Women have historically been involved in diaconate types of ministries, whether they were given the title *deacon* or *deaconess* or not. Although I think that there is scriptural warrant for female deacons, while maintaining male headship, it doesn't matter to me whether we're given the title or not. Any woman who wants to pick up the basin and the towel may do so, whether she's got a title or not. Phoebe was referred to as a "protectress of many," a title given to Roman citizens who cared for the needs of destitute aliens. Ponder the lives of Amy Carmichael, who served the destitute for fifty-six years in India, and Clara Barton, the founder of the American Red Cross, of whom it was said, "She was perhaps the most perfect incarnation of mercy the modern world had ever known."[11] My great-aunt, Beulah Watters, was a missionary in Hong Kong for her entire life. She founded an orphanage and gathered starving children from the dump to feed and care for.

I hope that by now you're feeling encouraged to seek out opportunities, whether in private or public, to use the years that the Lord has allotted you to continue to live for the benefit of others. Rather than looking at this time as a season of vacations and self-indulgence, why not press yourself for new opportunities for service? Whether you're an artist, radio show host, or just "Mimi" to some precious little souls, the church and the world need what you have to offer.

Unchangeable, Yet Changing All Things

> For who is Lord but our Lord? Or who is God besides our God? Most high, most excellent, most mighty, most omnipotent; most merciful and most just; most hidden and most near; most beautiful and most strong; constant, yet incomprehensible; unchangeable, yet changing all things; never new, never old; renewing all things, yet bringing old age upon the proud, without their knowing it; always working, yet always at rest. (St. Augustine)[12]

As we conclude, let me focus your attention where we began. Let's look heavenward, to see the God who is, as Augustine wrote, "constant, yet incomprehensible; unchangeable, yet changing all things; never new, never old."

We began thinking about the ways in which everything in creation changes—except our God. All stars and moons, all grass and trees, all life in every form is shifting, changing, becoming new and old, ending. We're in that process, too, changing, aging, becoming new, growing old. And yet there is one constant on whom we can rely. It's impossible that he might be altered. He is perfect now, as he always has been, and he won't ever change from that perfection or grow to become somehow better or more perfect. We can rely on him, as we have all these years, to be there, exactly as he has always been: loving and holy, merciful and just, filled with love and good plans for us. Be valiant, my sisters! He's nearer to us now than ever before!

1. What have you learned about areas of opportunity for service?

2. What do you think God is calling you to do?

3. As you think back over the experiences of your life, what can you offer to younger women that will encourage them?

4. Summarize what you've learned in this chapter.

5. Summarize what you've learned in this book.

Epilogue

Although an epilogue is defined as the "concluding part of a literary work"[1] (and that's what this short little *goodbye . . . for now* is), I hope that you've caught a vision in the preceding pages that what's left of your life shouldn't be thought of as your epilogue. I trust that you've come to see that this time of life, fraught with challenges as it is, is perfectly suited for you: a woman who's no longer focused on mere outward beauty or worried about the trifles of life but rather has become confident, wise, and valiant because of God's gracious work in her soul.

At this writing I'm fifty-two years old. I don't mind telling you that because I'm looking at my age as a sort of badge of honor. With the grace of the Lord, I've made it through the trials of my teen years and early marriage and motherhood; I've persevered through graduations and childbirths and heartache and great joys; I've skipped down paths lined with green pastures, and I've struggled to hold onto my Savior's hand as I've traversed the valley of the shadow of death. I've watched everyone around me change and grow, and I've seen change, growth, and yes, even aging, in myself. In the light of all this experience and variance, I have to say that I'm growing in the appreciation of this time in my life. I'm thankful that I don't have to worry any more about the kinds of things that troubled me when I was younger.

Please let me encourage you to interact with Scripture once again. This time, look at Psalm 23, a psalm that has become very precious to me especially through the afternoon hours:

> The LORD is my shepherd,
> I shall not want.
> He makes me lie down in green pastures;
> He leads me beside quiet waters.
> He restores my soul;
> He guides me in the paths of righteousness
> For His name's sake.
>
> Even though I walk through the valley of the shadow
> of death,
> I fear no evil, for you are with me;
> Your rod and Your staff, they comfort me.
> You prepare a table before me in the presence of my
> enemies;
> You have anointed my head with oil;
> My cup overflows.
> Surely goodness and lovingkindness will follow me all
> the days of my life,
> And I will dwell in the house of the LORD forever. (Ps.
> 23:1–6)

What does it mean to you that the Lord is your shepherd? Does it soothe your soul to remember our Lord called himself a good Shepherd (John 10:11)? It is the job of every shepherd to care for, feed, and guide his flock. "He takes us into his fold, and then takes care of us, protects us, and provides for us, with more care and constancy than a shepherd can, that makes it his business to keep the flock."[2] Because God has made caring for you his business, you can be sure that he won't let you want for any needful thing. He's the good Shepherd. "I shall be supplied with whatever I need; and, if I have not every thing I desire, I may conclude it is either not fit for me or not good for me or I shall have it in due time."[3] Hasn't he been a good Shepherd to you?

Do you need a place of rest and nourishment? He'll cause you to repose in lush pastures. Do you need to be refreshed? He'll enable you to sip contentedly from the sweet, tranquil waters of heaven. Does your soul need restoring? The one who created you knows how to place your soul back on the right path and cause it to flourish in wholeness and health.

Do you need guidance? This is a time of life when we need to know his leading. We need to learn how to relate differently to all our loved ones, to rejoice in the changes we observe in our bodies. The Lord's promise is sure: In every case and at all times, he'll instruct and illumine your heart through his Word and by the Spirit. What is your duty now? The Lord will make it plain for his own glory, and in that you can rest confidently.

Are you going through distressing times? Perhaps some of the troubles you've read about in this book are not merely knocking on your door but are breaking it down. Perhaps you're facing the heartache of children leaving or of the death of a beloved parent. There are times when I feel overcome by trials and would call myself anything but a valiant woman! It's then that I have to take myself back to this word that consoles me and brings me shelter. It's during these times that David's words encourage my heart: "Even though I walk through the valley of the shadow of death, I will fear no evil, for You are with me . . . you comfort me." The Lord is with us; he will not forsake us. We can rest on his guiding staff and rod. Feast on these comments by Matthew Henry on the "valley of the shadow of death":

> [1.] It is but the *shadow* of death; there is no substantial evil in it; the shadow of a serpent will not sting nor the shadow of a sword kill. [2.] It is the *valley* of the shadow, deep indeed, and dark, and dirty; but the valleys are fruitful, and so is death itself fruitful of comforts to God's people. [3.] It is but a *walk* in this valley, a gentle pleasant walk. The wicked are chased out of the world, and their souls are required; but the saints take a walk to another world as cheerfully as they take their leave of this. [4.] It is a walk *through* it; they shall not be lost in this valley, but get safely to the mountain of spices on the other side of it.[4]

> Even when we feel surrounded by foes, yes, even then, our faithful Lord will feed us from His table, soothe our minds with His anointing oil and prosper us so that we say, "Our cup overflows with goodness!" He will supply pardoning mercy, protecting mercy, sustaining mercy and supplying mercy![5]

All of this will be supplied to us not just now, in these afternoon days but also throughout all the remaining days of our lives. And what do we have to look forward to? What is our hope? Dwelling in the house of the Lord *forever!* Every hour we live here draws us one step closer to that house and to the mercy and goodness that will overcome all our sorrows and enrapture our hearts.

This time of life isn't the epilogue. *It's still the prologue,* the beginning of an eternity filled with pleasures beyond our imagination! So then, let us offer up our hearts, minds, hands, and bodies to be used as valiant women in his vineyard, while we eagerly anticipate the great joy that we'll know when our good Shepherd finally brings us home!

Notes

Introduction

1. Elyse Fitzpatrick and Carol Cornish, gen. eds., *Women Helping Women* (Eugene, OR: Harvest House, 1997).

Chapter 1: To Everything There Is a Time

1. Adam Clarke, *Clarke's Commentary,* electronic database, ©1996 by Biblesoft. All rights reserved.

2. Peter Kreeft, *Love Is Stronger Than Death* (San Francisco: Ignatius Press, 1992), xv.

3. John Calvin, *Heart Aflame* (Phillipsburg, NJ: P&R, 1999), 222.

4. Edward T. Welch, "Exalting Pain? Ignoring Pain? What Do We Do with Suffering?" *The Journal of Biblical Counseling* 12, no. 3 (spring 1994), 4.

5. Jay E. Adams, *Life Under the Son* (Stanley, NC: Timeless Texts, 1999), 30.

Chapter 2: The Valiant Afternoon Woman

1. Bruce K. Waltke, "The Role of the 'Valiant Wife' in the Marketplace," *Crux* 35 (1999): 23–34.

2. See also Pss. 19:7–11; 119:97–104, 130; Micah 2:7; Acts 20:20, 27.

3. First Peter 3:7 does state that the wife is a weaker vessel. "Weaker vessel" can and probably does mean several things. First, physically a woman is generally weaker than a man as far as brute force goes, although her muscles can withstand longer periods of use. She has less muscle mass and is less able to body build unless she takes steroids or male hormones. She is also

subject to menstrual cycles and hormonal changes, which weaken her physically. She is more dependent upon others due to her God-given ability to conceive, carry, and nurture a child, and therefore she is more reliant upon a man to protect and provide for her and her children. Finally, she is in a position of subordination in the marriage relationship, which makes her weaker or more vulnerable. I think that this is Peter's point, since the entire passage beginning with 1 Peter 2:18 teaches subordinates how to relate to those in authority over them. A husband needs to treat his wife with dignity and understanding because he is in a position of power over her and before the Lord she is his equal. If he fails to do this, Peter warns him, his prayers will be "hindered."

4. *New American Standard Hebrew Aramaic-Greek Dictionaries,* Libronix Digital Library System.

5. Al Wolters, *The Song of the Valiant Woman* (Carlisle, United Kingdom: Paternoster, 2001), 12. "The subject of the song is called an *'eset hayil,* a term which has been translated in many different ways, but which in this context should probably be understood as the female counterpart of the *gibbor hayil,* the title given to the 'mighty men of valor' which are often named in David's age. The person who is celebrated in this song is a 'mighty woman of valor' " (ibid., 9).

6. Some authors believe that this picture can't be that of a Christian woman because "the husband is left with little or nothing to do!" (Thomas P. McCreesh, "Wisdom as Wife: Proverbs 31:10–31," 27, in Waltke, "The Role of the 'Valiant Wife,' "). Through the ages, this woman has been allegorized as the Torah (by the rabbis), Scripture, and the church. Martin Luther, along with Phillip Melanchthon and John Calvin, all broke with this tradition. Waltke argues against allegorizing her: "With the Protestant insistence on *sensus literalis* the valiant wife has been traditionally interpreted as a real wife" (Waltke, "The Role of the 'Valiant Wife,' " 33).

7. Paul Humbert, "Entrendre la Main," *Vetus Testamentum* 12, no. 162, 187, quoted in Waltke, "The Role of the 'Valiant Wife,' " 25. I first became acquainted with this article when reading Carolyn Custis James, *When Life and Beliefs Collide* (Grand Rapids, MI: Zondervan, 2001).

8. She's dressed in fine linen and purple, the royal garments of priests and kings.

9. *New American Standard Hebrew Aramaic-Greek Dictionaries.*

10. *Sachaq* is the Hebrew for "laughs" and is frequently used as a war-like term to describe a victor's laughter at his enemy's defeat. " 'Watching over' (v. 27) glosses the normal Hebrew term for 'to reconnoiter' and 'to spy' " (KBL 3:1044, quoted in Waltke, "The Role of the 'Valiant Wife,' " 25).

11. "Keep Young and Beautiful," from *Forty-Second Street*, the musical, by Harry Warren and Al Dubin, Warner Brothers, 2001.

12. Edward T. Welch, *When People Are Big and God Is Small* (Phillipsburg, NJ: P&R, 1997), 97.

13. Waltke, "The Role of the 'Valiant Wife,' " 29.

Chapter 3: Just the Two of Us

1. See my discussion of this topic in Elyse Fitzpatrick, *Helper by Design* (Chicago: Moody Press, 2003), p. 34. In the Hebrew there are two ways to say that something is not good. The first way is to say that it is *en tob,* which means that something is lacking in good, like coffee without sugar. The other way to say it is *lo tob,* which means that it is positively bad, like drinking burned coffee grounds. The Hebrew here is *lo tob,* indicating that Adam's plight without an assistant who was like him was affirmatively bad.

2. That God loves distinctions is seen not only in the differences between man and woman but also in the distinctions that he maintains between the creation and himself and even within the roles of the Trinity.

3. "At the time of Lazarus's sickness and the sisters' call, Jesus was in Peraea beyond Jordan, on His way to Jerusalem, two days' journey from Bethany. He delayed two days to give time for that death which He foresaw, and from which He was about to raise Lazarus" (*Fausset's Bible Dictionary*, electronic database ©1998 by Biblesoft).

4. See Elyse Fitzpatrick and Carol Cornish, gen. eds., *Women Helping Women* (Eugene, OR: Harvest House, 1997).

Chapter 4: Don't Forget to Write

1. Dr. Peter Jones, in a chapel service at Westminster Theological Seminary in California. Unpublished chapel notes.

2. *Reader's Digest Oxford Complete Wordfinder* (Pleasantville, NY: Reader's Digest Association, Inc.), 1996.

3. Ibid.

4. Charles H. Spurgeon, *Spurgeon's Encyclopedia of Sermons,* "The Guilt and the Cleansing," a sermon delivered on Lord's day evening, January 8, 1865 by C. H. Spurgeon at the Metropolitan Tabernacle, Newington, (electronic database; Seattle: Biblesoft, 1997.

5. © Peacemaker® Ministries. Used by permission. For more information about biblical peacemaking, visit the Peacemaker Ministries web site at www.HisPeace.org or contact Peacemaker Ministries at 406/256–1583.

Chapter 5: Leaving Your Father and Mother

1. The premarital counseling I've done has been primarily with family friends as I've made it a general rule to limit my counseling to women.

2. Quoted from Wayne Mack and Nathan Mack, *Preparing for Marriage God's Way* (Tulsa, OK: Virgil W. Hensley, 1986), 33.

3. Jay E. Adams, *Solving Marriage Problems* (Grand Rapids, MI: Zondervan, 1983), 69.

4. John Piper, *Desiring God* (Sisters, OR: Multnomah, 1986), 224.

5. Ibid., 222.

Chapter 6: Just Call Me "Mimi"!

1. *Bible Dictionary,* copyright (c) 1994, Biblesoft and International Bible Translators, Inc.

2. *Grand-boomer* is AARP's designation for baby-boomer grandparents. Baby boomers were born between 1946 and 1964. From "The Grandparent Study 2002 Report," a research report ©AARP, May 2002.

3. Joni Eareckson Tada and Steven Estes, *When God Weeps* (Grand Rapids, MI: Zondervan, 2000).

4. Figures from the U.S. Census Bureau, year 2000 samples.

Chapter 8: Dear Unbelieving Child, How I Long for Your Soul

1. Tom Bisset, *Why Christian Kids Leave the Faith* (Nashville: Thomas Nelson, 1992).

Chapter 10: I'm Getting Comfortable with Looking Comfortable

1. Hysterectomy Status by State and Age, National Uterine Fibroids Foundation, Camarillo, California, 1998–2000.

2. There are numbers of books that outline homeopathic or more natural responses to menopause. These references do not represent a Christian worldview, and some of them suggest other quasi-spiritual remedies for the problems facing menopausal women. My recommendations come therefore with the advice that you might find some things helpful in them, but you must read with a deliberately critical eye. Among them are John R. Lee, M.D., with Virginia Hopkins, *What Your Doctor May Not Tell You About Menopause* (New York: Warner Books, 1996); Susan Love, M.D., with Karen Lindsey, *Dr. Susan Love's Hormone Book* (New York: Random House, 1997). Dr. Love's book outlines the many options available to the menopausal woman as well as furnishing the reader with a more historical perspective. See also Gayle Sand, *Is It Hot in Here or Is It Just Me? A Personal Look at the Facts, Fallacies, and Feelings of Menopause* (New York: Harper Collins, 1993).

3. Shirley V. Galucki, M. D., "Medical Questions Women Ask," in Elyse Fitzpatrick and Carol Cornish, gen. eds., *Women Helping Women* (Eugene, OR: Harvest House, 1997), 539.

4. Older women taking combination hormone therapy had twice the rate of dementia, including Alzheimer's disease, compared with women who did not take the medication, according to new findings from a memory substudy of the Women's Health Initiative. The research, part of the Women's Health Initiative Memory Study (WHIMS) and reported in the May 28, 2003, *Journal of the American Medical Association* (*JAMA*), found the heightened risk of developing dementia in a study of women sixty-five and older taking Prempro™, a particular form of estrogen plus progestin hormone therapy. (Internet article published by the National Institutes of Health, U.S. Department of Health and Human Services, May 27, 2003.)

5. Fitzpatrick and Cornish, *Women Helping Women*, 537.

6. *Physic* is an old English word for a medicine or drug.

7. Question 135, The Westminster Larger Catechism, *The Westminster Standards* (Suwanee, GA: Great Commission Publications, 1997), 57.

8. Fitzpatrick and Cornish, *Women Helping Women*, 458.

9. Al Wolters, *The Song of the Valiant Woman* (Carlisle, United Kingdom: Paternoster, 2001), 9.

10. Ibid, 11.

Chapter 11: Afternoon Women in Ministry

1. See Martha Peace, *Becoming a Titus 2 Woman* (Bemidji, Minn.: Focus Publishing, 1997), and Carolyn Mahaney, *Feminine Appeal* (Wheaton, IL: Crossway, 2003.

2. Enhanced Strong's Lexicon.

3. Ibid.

4. Mahaney, *Feminine Appeal,* 20.

5. There is some discussion about the identity of Lemuel, whether he was Solomon or another writer. This discussion doesn't bear on the truth that he learned about the characteristics of a godly woman from his mother, whether she was Bathsheba or another woman.

6. See Elyse Fitzpatrick and Carolyn Cornish, gen. eds., *Women Helping Women* (Eugene, OR: Harvest House, 1997).

7. See Elyse Fitzpatrick, *Helper by Design* (Chicago: Moody Press, 2003).

8. Thomas R. Schreiner, "The Ministries of Women in the Context of Male Leadership," in *Recovering Biblical Manhood and Womanhood,* ed. John Piper and Wayne Grudem (Wheaton, IL: Crossway, 1991), 210.

9. Ibid., 216.

10. *Matthew Henry's Commentary on the Whole Bible: New Modern Edition,* Electronic Database (Peabody, Mass.: Hendrickson, 1991).

11. The *Detroit Free Press,* upon the occasion of her death in 1912.

12. From *Restless Till We Rest in You,* Paul Thigpen, comp. (Ann Arbor, MI: Servant, 1998, 20); quoted from The Confessions 1.4.

Epilogue

1. *Reader's Digest Oxford Complete Wordfinder* (Pleasantville, NY: Reader's Digest Association, Inc.), 1996.

2. Matthew Henry, *Matthew Henry's Commentary on the Whole Bible* (Peabody, MA: Hendrickson, 1991).

3. Ibid.

4. Ibid.

5. Ibid.

About the Contributors

Vickie Daggett has been married twenty-eight years and has three grown children and one granddaughter. She serves as an administrator at Berean Bible College and counsels women at her church.

Karen Haney and her husband of thirty-one years live in Southern California and find much joy in their three sons, two daughters-in-law, and four grandchildren. She works with her husband in a small business that they own in the North San Diego County area.

Barbara Lerch has been married twenty-eight years, has four children, and one dachshund. She has worked for P&R Publishing for seventeen years, where she is an acquisitions editor/associate editor. She attends River of Life OPC in Phillipsburg, N.J. where she enjoys teaching junior high Sunday school and serves as a ladies group leader. She is delighted to be in the afternoon of life!

Anita Manata teaches fourth grade at The Classical Academy in Escondido, California. A member of Grace Bible Church in Escondido, Manata is involved in women's ministries. She has two sons and one grandson.

Kathie Printy lives in San Diego with her husband of thirty-eight years, Ted. They have four grown children and six grandchildren.

Kathie is active in women's and children's ministries at North City Presbyterian Church.

Eileen Scipione, with her husband George, brings her practical, pioneering spirit to all of the roles into which God has placed her. She has brought her commitments to the sufficiency of Scripture, the importance of family, the Reformed doctrines of grace, the belief that women should be counseling women, and the sanctity of human life from conception to natural death, to the front lines for many years. Eileen is the mother of five children: Paul, Ruth, Nicole, Arielle, and Deborah. She is a counselor at the Institute for Biblical Counseling and Discipleship in La Mesa, California.

Juliette Smith, a native San Diegan, attended San Diego State University briefly before marriage. She is retired from a career in the hospitality field/hotel development. Smith served as trustee for New Life Orthodox Presbyterian Church and was active with the San Diego Rescue Mission Auxiliary. Along with husband Bob, five children, and seven grandchildren, she enjoys backpacking, skiing, and river rafting.

About the Author

Elyse Fitzpatrick has been counseling women since 1989 and is a part-time counselor at the Institute for Biblical Counseling and Discipleship (www.ibcd.org). She holds a certificate in biblical counseling from IBCD and an M.A. in Biblical Counseling from Trinity Theological Seminary. Elyse is a member of the National Association of Nouthetic Counselors and a frequent speaker at women's conferences. She has written a number of books, including *Idols of the Heart*. Elyse has been married for nearly thirty years and has three adult children and four grandchildren.